Table Talk

Table Talk

Beginning the Conversation
on the Gospel of Mark
(Year B)

Jay Cormier

New City Press
Hyde Park, New York

For Father Peter Guerin, O.S.B.

Published in the United States by New City Press
202 Comforter Blvd., Hyde Park, NY 12538
www.newcitypress.com
©2011 Jay Cormier

Cover design by Durva Correia

Library of Congress Cataloging-in-Publication Data:

A copy of the CIP data is available from the Library of Congress

ISBN 978-1-56548-393-4

Printed in the United States of America

Contents

Introduction 9

Advent

First Sunday of Advent..13
Second Sunday of Advent 15
Third Sunday of Advent 17
Fourth Sunday of Advent 20

Christmas

Christmas: The Nativity of the Lord 25
    Mass of the Vigil 26
    Mass at Midnight...27
    Mass at Dawn 28
    Mass of the Day...29
The Holy Family 30
Sunday after Christmas 33
January 1 36
Epiphany..39
The Baptism of the Lord 42

Lent

Ash Wednesday 47
First Sunday of Lent..50
Second Sunday of Lent 53
Second Sunday of Lent 56
Third Sunday of Lent 59
Fourth Sunday of Lent...62
Fifth Sunday of Lent 65
Sunday of the Lord's Passion: Palm Sunday...............68
    The Blessing and Procession of Palms.................68
    The Passion of Our Lord Jesus.............................70

The Easter
Triduum

Holy Thursday...77
Good Friday..80
The Easter Vigil..82

Easter

Easter Sunday..87
Second Sunday of Easter...90
Third Sunday of Easter...94
Fourth Sunday of Easter...97
Fifth Sunday of Easter..99
Sixth Sunday of Easter..101
The Ascension of the Lord...104
Seventh Sunday of Easter..107
Pentecost..110

Solemnities of the Lord
in Ordinary Time

The Holy Trinity..115
The Body and Blood of the Lord.................................118

Ordinary Time

Second Sunday of the Year.. 123
Second Sunday after the Epiphany.............................. 125
Third Sunday of the Year /
    Third Sunday after Epiphany 127
Fourth Sunday of the Year /
    Fourth Sunday after Epiphany................................ 129
Fifth Sunday of the Year /
    Fifth Sunday after Epiphany 132
Sixth Sunday of the Year /
    Sixth Sunday after Epiphany................................. 135

Sunday 7 / Proper 2 138
Sunday 8 / Proper 3 141
Sunday 9 / Proper 4 144
Sunday 10 / Proper 5 147
Sunday 11 / Proper 6 150
Sunday 12 / Proper 7 153
Sunday 13 / Proper 8 155
Sunday 14 / Proper 9 158
Sunday 15 161
Proper 10 163
Sunday 16 / Proper 11 167
Sunday 17 / Proper 12 170
Sunday 18 / Proper 13 173
Sunday 19 / Proper 14 175
Sunday 20 / Proper 15 178
Sunday 21 / Proper 16 181
Sunday 22 / Proper 17 184
Sunday 23 / Proper 18 187
Sunday 24 / Proper 19 190
Sunday 25 / Proper 20 194
Sunday 26 / Proper 21 197
Sunday 27 / Proper 22 200
Sunday 28 / Proper 23 203
Sunday 29 / Proper 24 206
Sunday 30 / Proper 25 209
Sunday 31 / Proper 26 212
Sunday 32 / Proper 27 214
Sunday 33 218
Proper 28 221
Christ the King / The Reign of Christ [Proper 29] 224

Notes.. 227

Introduction

*T*his book is designed to begin a *conversation,* a conversation that takes place each Sunday at the table of the Lord.

The conversation begins with a particular memory of the extraordinary life of the Gospel Jesus: a story he told, a wonder he worked; a confrontation with the establishment, a misunderstanding with his disciples; remembering when he cried, when he despaired, when he was abandoned, when he got angry; the injustice of his condemnation, the horror of his death, the vindication of his resurrection.

The conversation then seeks to understand what this memory of Jesus means to us in the marketplaces and temples of our time and place. In word and sacrament, we share the wonders of healing and forgiveness that Jesus is performing in our midst.

It's a conversation that shows no signs of being exhausted.

It is the writer's hope that these pages will provoke *Table Talk* — reflection and insight about the God's Word as it is proclaimed at the table of the Lord on Sunday. The focus here is on the Sunday Gospel — the climactic reading at the Sunday Eucharist in which God speaks to us, touches us, loves us in the story of Jesus, God's Christ, *Emmanuel.*

The reflections offered here are one poor pilgrim's attempt to grasp the Gospel after many journeys through the lectionary as a writer, teacher and struggling disciple. These essays are intended to help spark the Sunday conversation around your parish table: to be starting points for the homilist who will preach on the Gospel, the catechist who will teach that Gospel to children, the RCIA team who will lead candidates through a discussion of the passage, or the individual disciple looking for a companion on his/her day-to-day journey to Emmaus.

(This volume follows both the pericopes of both the Roman Catholic lectionary and the "common" lectionary used by many Protestant churches. Where different Gospel readings are assigned, reflections on each reading are offered.)

The problem with a collection like this is that it might be perceived as a final word, a definitive reading, a complete analysis of the Sunday Gospel reading. This book is no such thing. It is one "converser's" reflection and best reading of these Gospel stories after many years of his own prayer, reflection and teaching. Perhaps you will find here few nuggets of gold from a very deep mine; more gifted and wiser miners will find much more of value as they dig deeper and deeper.

If this book helps you begin that conversation at your own table this Sunday or helps you in your own search and study, these pages will have done their job.

ADVENT

First Sunday of Advent

"Be watchful! Be alert! You do not know when the time will come."

Mark 13: 33–37

Every precious Advent moment

Anyone who has lived with cancer or AIDS or some life-threatening disease will tell you the same thing: Every tick of your watch, every second that flashes by on your desk clock is precious.

Those who survive a cardiac event will readily share with you the valuable lesson their illness has taught them: Every hour of every day is a bonus.

They will explain how you learn to prize people, how you understand that they can be as fragile and fearful as you have been.

And you don't grasp at things, because, after all, the Creator didn't close his hand on you but let you sit quietly, like a butterfly, on his own palm.

Every walk in the woods becomes an encounter with the sacred.

Every hour spent with your spouse and children and grandchildren and friends become special.

Every moment spent with another person becomes too important to waste on recriminations and pettiness, on judgments and rejections. You don't quarrel anymore; you discuss.

Even though you are the one who deserves compassion, you develop the rare ability to offer compassion to friends and loved ones.

Every choice you make is made with great care — from what you will have for dinner to what book you will read. Joy, peace, and reconciliation are the driving forces in your life.

Once you realize that your exit from life's stage has been scripted, once you understand that your time is finite and limited, once you accept the reality that "later" is "now" and "tomorrow" is "today," every experience is cherished, every moment is lived with gratitude.

Advent confronts us with the preciousness and limits of time — that our lives are an Advent, a prelude, to the life of God to come. While confronting us with the reality that our lives are finite and fragile, these Sundays of Advent also assure us of the mercy of God, who is with us in the midst of all of the struggles and challenges of our everyday Advent journey to the dwelling place of God.

The beginning of the Christian year begins at the end — the promised return of Christ at the end of time. In today's brief Gospel parable of the master's return, Jesus articulates the Advent themes of waiting, watchfulness and readiness. Jesus calls us to realize our responsibilities in the present as we dare to look forward to the promise of the future.

Jesus calls us to realize what the terminally ill understand: that this life of ours is a precious, limited gift. Advent calls us to "stay awake" and not sleep through the opportunities life gives us to discover God in the love of others. Advent urges us to "watch," to pay attention to the signs of God's unmistakable presence in our lives, to live life expectantly not as a death sentence but as a gift from God.

*F*ather, Giver of this precious and wonderful life
  of ours,
wake us up to the preciousness of every moment
  you give us.
Do not let us sleep through the Advent we live every day.
May Christ's coming shake us awake
that we may come to know you in the love of others
and the goodness of this world you have given us.

People of the whole Judean countryside and all the inhabitants of Jerusalem were being baptized by John in the Jordan River as they acknowledged their sins.

Mark 1: 1–8

The work of the Baptizer

*T*is the season of Santa and Kris Kringle.

We are all working very hard to be Santa for those we love — or to be good enough for Santa to come down our chimneys this Christmas with that perfect gift.

Or we might be someone's Kris Kringle or "secret Santa" this Christmas: We may have chosen the name of a member of our family or classmate or fellow worker for whom we will try to make this Christmas a little merrier.

Being Santa or Kris Kringle can be hard but fulfilling work; we can receive as much as we give in our Santa-playing.

But every Advent our Gospel readings center on this strange, austere, humorless character John the Baptizer. The Baptizer of the Gospels is nobody's idea of Christmas joy: subsisting on locusts and wild honey, clad in camel hair, haunting a wild river bank. We happily take on the role of Kris Kringle, but we just don't see ourselves as John.

But that is exactly who Advent calls us to be. In our own baptisms we promised to become "Baptizers" along our own Jordan Rivers. So embrace the work of the Baptizer this Christmas; take on the call to be a herald like John as we go about our holiday preparations:

- may we give the gifts of "comfort" and joy;
- may our Christmas cards express the hope and good news of Christ's coming;

- may every kindness and generosity we extend this Christmas mirror Christ's presence in our midst;
- may we joyfully take on the hard work of creating a highway through the rugged lands of estrangement and alienation;
- may the gifts and greetings and hospitality we extend proclaim the good news that God's compassion had dawned.

John's brief appearance in Mark's Gospel begins a new era in the history of salvation. Mark's details about John's appearance recall the austere dress of the great prophet Elijah (2 Kings 1: 8). The Jews believed that Elijah would return from heaven to announce the long-awaited restoration of Israel as God's kingdom. For Mark and the synoptics, this expectation is fulfilled in John the Baptizer. In the Baptizer's proclamation of Jesus as the Messiah, the age of the prophets is fulfilled and the age of the Messiah begins. As an "Advent people," we are caught (like the Israelites returning to Jerusalem in today's first reading from Isaiah) between a world that is dying and, at the same time, a world waiting to be reborn. The work of Advent is to bring about that rebirth: to prepare a world that is ready for the Lord's coming.

In our own baptisms, we take on the role of prophet of the Christ. The word *prophet* comes from the Greek word meaning "one who proclaims." In our baptismal call to become prophets of the God who comes, we take on the prophetic work of transforming the wastelands around us into harvests of justice and forgiveness, to create highways for our God to enter and re-create our world in charity and peace.

*T*his Christmas, O God,
may we become prophets of your Christ's coming.
May our gifts of compassion and healing,
our lights of welcome and hope,
our songs of joy and peace proclaim to waiting hearts
that you have come.

John was sent from God to testify to the light, so that all might believe through him.

"I am 'the voice of one crying out in the desert, make straight the way of the Lord ... '

"I baptize with water; but there is one among you whom you do not recognize, the one who coming after me ... "

John 1: 6–8, 19–28

Christmas in Greccio

Keeping Christ in Christmas is not a new challenge. Trying to capture the real meaning of this holy season despite the commercialism has been a problem for close to a millennium. In 1223, Francis of Assisi took up the challenge — and gave us a cherished tradition.

What Francis wanted to do was help people "see with our bodily eyes ... what [Jesus] suffered for lack of the necessities of a newborn Babe and how He lay in a manger between an ox and an ass." So, with the help of his friend, landowner Giovanni Velita, Francis constructed a manger, filled it with hay and brought in an ox and an ass from a local farm. Then Francis and his brothers extended an invitation to all the people of the town to come to the manger on Christmas Eve. Lights were kindled, songs and hymns were sung, and Mass was celebrated in the manger itself, with Deacon Francis singing the Gospel of Christ's birth. The saint then preached about the birth of the poor King, the Babe of Bethlehem. Simplicity was honored, poverty exalted, humility praised.

Contrary to popular belief, there were no statues of the Holy Family or shepherds or angels nor did Francis recruit "live actors" to play any of those parts. The people gathered to pray in a place of simple poverty like the place in which God touched human history.

Francis' ramshackle manger captured the simple poverty of the time and place in which God entered our human world.

"Greccio was transformed into a second Bethlehem," Francis' biographer, Thomas of Celano, writes, "and that wonderful night seemed like fullest day to both man and beast for the joy they felt at the renewing of the mystery."

Both John the Baptizer at the Jordan River and Francis in the manger he re-created that Christmas night in Greccio proclaim the same joyful news of the manger: *God is with us.* God has revealed himself to his people through the Incarnation of his Word, Jesus the Christ. In today's Gospel, John the Baptizer points to this revelation as standing "among you whom you do not recognize."

Forms of "baptism" were common in the Judaism of Gospel times — in some Jewish communities, it was through baptism rather than circumcision that a Gentile became a Jew. But John's baptism was distinctive: His baptism at the Jordan was a rite of repentance and *metanoia* — a conversion of heart and spirit. The Baptizer's ministry fulfilled the promise of Ezekiel (Ezekiel 36: 25–26): that, at the dawn of a new age, the God of Israel would purify his people from their sins with clear water and instill in them a new heart and spirit.

Advent faith calls us to approach God not in fear but in joy. Such faith is not a Pollyanna, happy-face, sugar-coated denial of whatever is bad or unpleasant, but a constant awareness that, despite the sufferings and difficulties of life, God is always present to us; that despite the heartaches, there is always healing; that despite our forgetting and abandoning God, God neither forgets nor abandons us; that despite the cross, there is the eternal hope of resurrection. In our own individual Advents of poverty and despair, God is with us; in our struggle to find meaning and purpose in this life we have been given, God is with us; in the humility and humiliations we endure, in the messes we make of our lives and the messes others make of their lives that we have to clean up, God is with us.

*C*ome, Lord God, into our Advent lives.
Illuminate our stables with your peace;
fill our poverty with your justice;
heal our brokenness with your forgiveness.
Despite our doubts and failings,
may we proclaim your compassion in our midst
and give voice to your love among us.

Fourth Sunday of Advent

"Hail, full of grace! The Lord is with you … Do not be afraid, Mary, for you have found favor with God. Behold, you shall conceive in your womb and bear a son, and you shall name him Jesus."

Mary said, "Behold, I am the handmaid of the Lord. May it be done to me according to your word."

Luke 1: 26–38

Everyday annunciations

She had not talked to her friend for some time and wondered how she was doing. She had heard that the family was going through a tough time. One morning, she saw that a movie they both said they were looking forward to seeing had opened. So she called her: "Hi. Would you like to take in a movie this afternoon?" After a pause, her friend said, "You know, that would be great. It would give us a chance to talk."

Hail, full of grace! The Lord is with you. You have found favor with God.

After her father died after a long, hard struggle with Alzheimer's Disease, she began making an annual gift to the Alzheimer's Association. One day she received a call asking if she would help organize a "memory walk" for Alzheimer's research. Her eyes fell on the photo of her Dad on her desk. "Yes, I'd love to help."

The Holy Spirit will come upon you and the power of God will overshadow you.

She is a college junior, majoring in education. The department chair asked her to stop by. "A downtown church is organizing an after-school program for at-risk kids," he explained. "They've asked if any of our students could serve as tutors. You have a real gift for working with young kids and you're going to make a great teacher. So I thought of you immediately." She asked a lot of questions; she wondered how she could work it into her busy class schedule; and she didn't have anywhere near the confidence in herself that her professor clearly had. But, in the end, she said: "I'd like to do it."

I am the handmaid of the Lord. May it be done.

In the Gospel for this Sunday before Christmas, God begins the "Christ event" with Mary, a simple Jewish girl who is at the very bottom of her society's social ladder; the God who created all things makes the fulfillment of his promise dependent upon one of the most dispossessed and powerless of his creatures. Luke's account of the angel Gabriel's appearance to Mary is filled with First Testament imagery (e.g., the announcement by the angel parallels the announcements of the births of many key figures in salvation history, such as Isaac and Samuel; the "overshadowing" of Mary recalls the cloud of glory covering the tent of the ark and temple in Jerusalem). Mary's yes to Gabriel's words sets the stage for the greatest event in human history: God's becoming human.

It may seem that formal "annunciations" are made only to Mary and other heroic, saintly figures in the Bible — but the fact is that God calls every one of us to the vocation of prophet, to the ministry of charity, to the work of forgiveness. Gabriel may come in the form of a request, an invitation, a plea, concern for another's well-being. Like Mary, we think of all kinds of reasons why this doesn't make any sense or that this task is beyond us — but it is in these everyday annunciations that God changes the course of history. In the Advents of our lives, God calls us to bring his Christ into our own time and place; may we respond with the faith and trust of Mary, putting aside our own doubts and fears to say *I am your servant, O God. Be it done.*

*G*racious God,
as Mary said "yes" to your word to her
    to give birth to your Son,
may we say "yes" to your word to us
to give birth to him in our own time and place.

May we create a dwelling place for him
in our works of charity and reconciliation.
May we give birth to him
in every word of consolation and support we speak,
in every joy we bring into the lives of others.
May we reveal his presence in our midst
in our efforts to bring your peace and justice
into our own Bethlehems and Nazareths.

CHRISTMAS

Preparing the stable

*B*arns and stables are fascinating places where every dimension of life and death are played out.

While children find barns exciting places of discovery and wonderful places to play, for farmers and ranchers they are places of hard work, anxiety and struggle. Within the rough planks of any barn, the new calf is born, young chicks are nurtured, the sick colt is cared for. It is the shelter for animals and the storehouse of the harvest, where hay is stacked, eggs are collected and milk is gathered.

Barns and stables are also filled with the grit and stench that are part of life. They are among the messiest and dirtiest of places. They warehouse old, tired and useless things — from obsolete tools to irreparably broken vehicles — until they are long forgotten.

And yet, in the Christmas moment, God transforms a cave used as a barn, a stable in a small backwater town, into the holiest of shrines, the most sacred of places.

In so many ways, our lives are stables of a kind, filled with every joy and pain and tension and mess necessary for us to grow, to learn, to develop, to fulfill our dreams and hopes. The Christ who is born in a Bethlehem stable comes to bring light and life to the stables that are each one of us. In Christ's birth, every human heart is born again and again and again.

Writing of his first Christmas as a Trappist monk at the Abbey of Our Lady of Gethsemani in Kentucky, Thomas Merton wrote:

"Christ always seeks the straw of the most desolate cribs to make his Bethlehem. In all the other Christmases of my life, I had got a lot of presents and a big dinner. This Christmas I got no presents, and not much of a dinner; but I would have, indeed, Christ, God, the Savior of the world.

"You who live in the world: let me tell you that there is no comparing these two kinds of Christmases ... the emptiness that had opened up within me, that had been prepared during Advent and laid open by my own silence and darkness, now became filled. And suddenly I was in a new world ...

"You know that Christ is born within you, infinite liberty: that you are free! That there are enemies which can never touch you, if this liberty loves you, and lives within you! That there are no more limitations! That you can love! That you are standing at the threshold of infinite possibilities!"[1]

The true miracle of Christmas continues to take place in the Bethlehems of our hearts. The trappings that surround this day, for the most part, do not begin to capture the profound meaning of the Christmas event. In the emptiness of our souls, God forgives us, reassures us, exalts us, lifts us up, loves us. In the coming of Jesus, God's love frees us, opening our hearts and spirits to new hope and possibilities. May we come to know this "kind" of Christmas — a Christmas when Christ fills the hearts we have emptied in order to make room for him.

The lectionary for Christmas provides four pericopes to celebrate the dawning of God's peace in a stable at Bethlehem:

Mass of the Vigil

"Joseph, son of David, do not be afraid to take Mary your wife into your home. For it is through the Holy Spirit that this child has been conceived in her."

Matthew 1: 1–25 [18–25]

*F*or Matthew, the story of Jesus begins with the promise to Abraham: that Jesus is the ultimate and perfect fulfillment of the Law and Prophets. So Matthew begins his Gospel with "a family record" of Jesus, tracing the infant's birth from Abraham (highlighting his Jewish identity) and David (his Messiahship). The accuracy of Matthew's list is dubious; but presenting an historic record is not the evangelist's point. Matthew proclaims in his genealogy that this Jesus is the fulfillment of a world that God envisioned from the first moment of creation — a world created in the justice and peace that is the very nature of its Creator.

Matthew's version of Jesus' birth follows. While Luke's account of Jesus' conception and birth centers around Mary, Joseph is the central figure in Matthew's account. In Matthew's story, Mary is found to be pregnant; her hurt and confused fiancé (who realizes he is not the father) is at a loss as to what to do. Joseph, an observant but compassionate Jew, decides to divorce Mary "quietly" to protect her from the full fury of the Law. But an angel appears to Joseph in a dream and reveals that this child is the fulfillment of Isaiah's prophecy. Putting aside his hurt and placing his trust in God's promise, Joseph acknowledges the child and names him *Jesus* ("Savior") and becomes, in the eyes of the Law, the legal father of Jesus. Because of Joseph's love and compassion for Mary, the Spirit of God sets into motion the dawning of the Christ.

The theme of Matthew's infancy narrative is *Emmanuel* — that Jesus is the promised Christ of old. Isaiah's prophecy has finally been fulfilled in Jesus: the virgin has given birth to a son, one who is a descendant of David's house (through Joseph). Jesus is truly *Emmanuel* — "God is with us."

Mass at Midnight

"For today in the city of David a savior has been born to you who is Christ and Lord."

Luke 2: 1–14

Centuries of hope in God's promise have come to fulfillment: the Messiah is born!

Luke's account of Jesus' birth begins by placing the event during the reign of Caesar Augustus. Augustus, who ruled from 27 B.C. until 14 A.D., was honored as "savior" and "god" in ancient Greek inscriptions. His long reign was hailed as the *pax Augusta* — a period of peace throughout the vast Roman world. Luke deliberately points out that it is during the rule of Augustus — the savior, god and peace-maker — that Jesus the Christ, the long-awaited Savior and Messiah, the Son of God and Prince of Peace, enters human history.

Throughout Luke's Gospel, it is the poor, the lowly, the outcast and the rejected who immediately embrace the preaching of Jesus. The announcement of the Messiah's birth to shepherds — who were among the most isolated and despised in the Jewish community — reflects Luke's theme that the poor are the blessed of God.

Mass at Dawn

"Let us go, then, to Bethlehem to see this thing that has taken place which the Lord has made known to us."

Luke 2: 15–20

*T*ypical of Luke's Gospel, it is the shepherds of Bethlehem — among the poorest and most disregarded of Jewish society — who become the first messengers of the Gospel.

From the Christmas story in Luke's Gospel, we have developed a romantic image of shepherds as gentle, peaceful figures. But that manger scene image is a far cry from the reality: The shepherds of Biblical times were tough, earthy characters who fearlessly used their clubs to defend their flocks from wolves and other wild animals. They had even less patience for the pompous scribes and Pharisees who treated them as second- and third-class citizens, barring these ill-bred rustics from the synagogue and courts.

Yet it was to shepherds that God first revealed the birth of the Messiah. The shepherds' vision on the Bethlehem hillside proclaims to all people of every place and generation that Christ comes for the sake of all of humankind.

The Gospel for the Mass at dawn ends with the touching detail: "And Mary kept all things, reflecting on them in her heart."

Mass of the Day

And the Word became flesh and made his dwelling among us ...

John 1: 1–18

*T*he Gospel for Christmas Day is the beautiful Prologue hymn to John's Gospel. With echoes of Genesis 1 ("In the beginning . . ," "the light shines on in darkness ..."), the Prologue exalts Christ as the creative Word of God that comes as the new light to illuminate God's re-creation.

In the original Greek text, the phrase "made his dwelling place among us" is more literally translated as "pitched his tent or tabernacle." The image evokes the Exodus memory of the tent pitched by Israelites for the Ark of the Covenant. God sets up the tabernacle of the new covenant in the body of the Child of Bethlehem.

The reading from John reminds us that Christmas is more than the birth of a child; it is the beginning of the Christ event that will transform and re-create human history, a presence that continues to this day and for all time. In this child, the extraordinary love of God has taken our "flesh" and "made his dwelling among us." In his "Word made flesh," God touches us at the very core of our beings, perfectly expressing his constant and unchanging love.

*I*n the birth of your Son, O God,
you have touched human history.
May the dawning of your Christ illuminate
    every morning;
may his birth re-create every human heart;
may his presence among us transform
    our stables and Bethlehems
into holy places of your compassion and peace.

"Behold, this child is destined for the fall and rise of many in Israel, and to be a sign that will be contradicted ... "

Luke 2: 22–40
[Roman lectionary]

The parents of the bride

*T*hey sit together in the front pew, the mother and father of the bride, holding and squeezing the other's hand tightly throughout the wedding service. They share smiles and not a few tears as their beloved daughter begins a new life with her husband, a terrific guy they already love as their own son.

As the liturgy unfolds, they cannot help but see more than just a beautiful bride in an exquisite gown: They also see the beautiful baby they brought home after a difficult pregnancy and an anything-but-easy delivery ... the four-year-old terrified by a thunderstorm or a bad dream, crawling into their bed with them ... the six-year-old triumphantly sounding out the words in her first-grade reader ... the 13-year-old on the threshold of womanhood ... the moody 16-year-old perpetually exasperated at her uncool parents' inability to understand anything ... the 18-year-old off to college and her first taste of freedom — and its costs ... the 22-year-old taking her first steps in the world of adult responsibility.

It was an exciting, fun, terrifying ride, this adventure in parenthood. But the child they nurtured with love, wisdom, compassion, conviction, and forgiveness has blossomed into a beautiful woman — ready now to begin the same ride herself.

Mary and Joseph begin their ride as parents by bringing their newborn son to the temple to present him to the Lord, to incorporate him into the life and traditions of their faith. Like everything that is good and of value in our lives, parenthood demands work and struggle. Today's Gospel is a sober reminder of that reality.

The faithful Joseph and Mary bring their son to the temple for his presentation to the Lord, a ritual required by the Law. The Book of Exodus taught that a family's first-born son "belonged" to the Lord who saved them when the first-born sons of the Egyptians were destroyed that night of Passover (Exodus 13: 15).

The prophet Simeon and the prophetess Anna are idealized portraits of the faithful "remnant" of Israel awaiting the Messiah's coming. Simeon's canticle praises God for the universal salvation that will be realized in Jesus; in his prophecy, the shadow of the cross falls upon the Holy Family. Anna, as an elderly widow, is considered among the most vulnerable and poor of society. Her encounter with the child typifies the theme woven throughout Luke's Gospel: the exaltation of society's poorest and most humble by God.

In Matthew and Luke's stories of Jesus' birth and childhood (which were later additions to those Gospels, drawn from the many stories about Jesus' life that were part of the early Christian oral tradition that had developed after his resurrection), life for the family of Joseph, Mary and Jesus is difficult and cruel: they are forced from their home; they are innocent victims of the political and social tensions of their time; they endure the suspicions of their own people when Mary's pregnancy is discovered; their child is born under the most difficult and terrifying of circumstances; they experience the agony of losing their beloved child. And yet, through it all, their love for and faithfulness to one another do not waver. The Holy Family is a model for our families as we confront the many tensions and crises that threaten the stability, peace and unity that are the joys of being a family.

Terrified and excited like most parents, Mary and Joseph seek to give their son the best they have — the faith and its values they cherish. We seek to give our own children the best that we have, as well. In baptism, we incorporate our sons and daughters into the life of the Risen Christ; within our home, we try to guide them in learning the Gospel values of compassion, love, forgiveness, justice and peace that we have embraced.

*L*oving Father,
keep our family within the embrace
    of your loving providence.
In times of crisis and tension,
bless our families with the hope of your consolation
    and forgiveness;
in times of joy and growth,
bless us with a spirit of thankfulness,
never letting us forget that you are Father of us all,
the Giver of all that is good.

Sunday after Christmas

And the Word became flesh and made his dwelling among us ...

John 1: 1–18
[Common lectionary]

'Joyeux Noel'

*I*t happened on Christmas Eve, 1914, during the first World War:

Three regiments — one French, one Scottish, and one German — were locked in battle on a French hillside. For weeks they had been annihilating one another from their dirty, cold trenches. Then, on Christmas Eve, an official truce was called and hostilities died down. A German soldier — a renowned opera singer before the war — began to sing *Silent Night* for his comrades. Suddenly, from the other side of the battle field, two Scottish bagpipes picked up the melody; then the pipers began to play *Adeste Fidelis,* and the tenor began to sing along with them. Soon soldiers from each side peered over No Man's Land and cautiously approached one another. Slowly, tentatively, the troops on both sides laid down their weapons and observed the birth of the Savior in whose name they were killing each other.

The story of this remarkable cease-fire is beautifully told in the French film *Joyeux Noel.*

Before long, the troops were standing together on the battlefield exchanging photographs of wives and girlfriends and sharing precious bits of chocolate and champagne. A priest from the Scottish regiment offered Mass in the cold field and all three regiments joined in prayer. The cease-fire was extended into Christmas Day, when the two sides happily skirmished in a soccer game. French, Scottish and German soldiers then helped one another to bury their dead whose bodies had been rotting on the cold, broken earth.

When the war resumed late on Christmas, none of the three sides could draw weapons against the others, for they could no longer see the other sides as enemies — they were now and forever fellow fathers and sons and farmers and artists and clerks. Christmas had transformed them into brothers.

When the general staffs of the three armies learned what had happened, the officers of the three regiments were reprimanded and the soldiers were punished for fraternizing. The French and English regiments were disbanded; the Germans were sent to the eastern front to fight the Russians.

The Scottish priest who celebrated the Christmas Eve Mass was severely admonished by his bishop, who ordered the priest back to his parish in Scotland immediately.

The priest pleaded, "I belong with those who are in pain and who have lost their faith. I belong here."

"I sincerely believe," the priest said, "that our Lord Jesus Christ guided me in what was the most important Mass of my life. I tried to be true to his trust and carry his message to all, whoever they may be."

But the bishop would not hear of it. "Those men who listened to you on Christmas Eve will very soon bitterly regret it because in a few days' time their regiment will be disbanded by order of His Majesty the King. Where will those poor boys end up on the front line now? And what will their families think?"

The bishop then dismissed the priest: "May our Lord Jesus Christ guide your steps back to the straight and narrow path."

"Is that truly the path of the Lord?" the devastated priest asked.

The bishop replied, "You're not asking the right questions."

The coming of Christ changes the questions. The dawning of Christ illuminates our perspective of the world and of one another. The coming of Christ transforms the hopeless and cynical winter landscape into a new springtime when peace is not only possible but imperative. Christmas is not just a cease-fire on our busy calendars but the transforming moment when God re-creates our humanity in his compassion and justice, a love that becomes real in the Child born this night.

The Gospel for this first Sunday after Christmas is the beautiful Prologue hymn to John's Gospel. With echoes of Genesis 1

("In the beginning ... ," "the light shines on in darkness ... "), the Prologue exalts Christ as the creative Word of God that comes as the new light to illuminate God's re-creation. In the original Greek text, the phrase "made his dwelling place among us" is more accurately translated as "pitched his tent or tabernacle." The image evokes the Exodus memory of the tent pitched by Israelites for the Ark of the Covenant. God sets up the tabernacle of the new covenant in the body of the Child of Bethlehem.

At Christmas, the sacred is no longer some abstract concept of theological theory; God has descended from the heavens to become one of us in order to show us how we might become like him. The love of God takes on a human face; the Word of God becomes "enfleshed" in the child Christ, enabling us to transform our hearts in that love and re-create our world in that Word of justice and compassion. This child is the very light of God, who inspires hearts and spirits to welcome all children as gifts of God, to find joy and completeness in loving our beloved, to care for the poorest and neediest creature as if he or she is Christ himself.

In Christ's birth, God touches human history: hope reigns, justice takes root, peace is possible. The challenge to each one of us is to take on the work of *Emmanuel*: to make God's presence tangible by being his "arms" for the hurting, his "hands" to the needy, his "heart" for the grieving.

*C*hrist Jesus,
you are the Word that set all of creation into motion;
you are the Light that illuminates every human life;
you are the love of God in flesh and blood.
Let your Word echo in our hearts
that we may re-create the world
   in the Father's compassion;
let your light shatter the darkness of sin and alienation;
let your love be the glory we seek,
as we struggle to imitate
your example of humble and grateful service
   to one another.

January 1

Mary the Mother of God
[Roman lectionary]

The Holy Name of Jesus
[Common lectionary]

When eight days were completed for his circumcision, he was named Jesus ...

Luke 2: 16–21

Shepherds and kings

*E*very one of our lives is depicted in the Christmas Gospels of Matthew and Luke.

Maybe you identify especially with the magi in the Epiphany story. Like the mysterious Eastern travelers, you are searching for meaning and purpose in your life; you are seeking something greater and more lasting that you are not finding in your profession or career. Follow the star to the Christ of the selflessness and justice.

Or maybe you are a shepherd, struggling to make a life for yourself and your family. You want your simple work and efforts to mean something, to be appreciated, to be respected. You seek only the dignity that rightfully belongs to every human being. Listen to the angels' news. Come to Bethlehem and welcome the Christ who has come to make you like him.

There may be a bit of Herod in you — not a murder streak like the despot in the Gospel, but maybe you are so consumed with your own pursuit of power and wealth, so overwhelmed with your own angers and jealousies that you destroy the lives and dreams of others who get in your way. If there is some of the Herod in you, take off your crown, come down from the throne you have built for yourself and meet the King who possesses real power.

If you live in a place like Bethlehem, rejoice in the good things that even a small place can accomplish out of the love of God. If you are a Jerusalem power-broker, remember that Christ is in your midst in the poor, the needy, the abandoned, the abused.

Remember that Mary and Joseph are your family, too, and that their Child is your newborn brother.

The Christmas and Epiphany stories speak to all of us of a God who so loves the world he fashioned that he entered that world in the most humble and hidden way imaginable so that the world may be transformed in such love. Whether we are a shepherd or a king, whether we struggle to eke out a living in Bethlehem or move among the powerful in Jerusalem, God invites us to follow the star, to behold the Child and to let the holiness and compassion manifested in him illuminate our lives with joy and hope.

On the threshold of a new calendar year, the Gospels for January 1 invite us, as does Mary in the midst of all that has happened in Bethlehem, to "reflect" in our own hearts what has taken place in the birth of this Child.

In the Roman Catholic tradition, today's solemnity honors Mary under her most ancient title — *Theotokos,* "Bearer of God": In accepting her role as mother of the Messiah, she becomes the first disciple of her Son, the first to embrace his Gospel of hope, compassion and reconciliation. As Mary, the young unmarried pregnant girl, believes and trusts in the incredible thing that she is to be a part of, even the most ordinary of us can believe in our parts in the drama, too.

In other traditions, January 1 honors the Holy Name of Jesus. Today's liturgy centers on the Gospel account of Jesus' circumcision at which he is given the name *Jesus* — "The Lord saves" — a name that not only identifies him but also marks the life he will live for the sake of humanity. It is the name we take on in our baptismal commitment to live the life of his Gospel. By his name, we are called to "give birth" to God in the stables and barns of our own time and place. "The Lord saves" in every work of compassion and mercy we extend, in the peace and justice we struggle to bring to our own Bethlehems and Nazareths and Jerusalems.

*F*ather of compassion,
in baptism we are reborn in the life of your Son;
we take on his name:
Jesus, "The Lord saves";
Christ, "the anointed of God."
May we live that name every day of this New Year:
may we create a dwelling place for you
in our works of charity and reconciliation;
may we give birth to you
in every word of consolation and support we speak,
in every joy we bring into the lives of others.

Epiphany

Magi from the east arrived in Jerusalem, saying, "Where is the newborn king of the Jews? We saw his star at its rising and have come to do him homage."

Matthew 2: 1–12

Finding God within

*T*he congregation was very proud of their beautiful church, which had stood proudly on the New England village common for generations. But, one night just before Thanksgiving, a spark in the heating system ignited a fire that destroyed the New England clapboard structure. Fortunately, no one was hurt, but the congregation was devastated. As soon as the fire marshal gave the all-clear, the devastated pastor and parishioners combed the rubble to salvage the few things they could.

Then, interesting things began to happen.

A nearby church — a congregation that the displaced congregation had little to do with before — offered them the use of their religious education building for services and meetings for as long as they needed it. Churches from nearby towns offered hymnals and other supplies; several churches took up a special collection for the congregation.

At the first service following the fire, the members of the congregation, who were used to sitting in his or her "own" place at a comfortable distance from one another, found themselves sitting side-by-side on folding chairs. After the service, teams started to form to deal with insurance, organize temporary arrangements for parish programs and religious education, and sketch out preliminary plans for a new church. The pastor tapped the expertise of everyone in the parish to help — and everyone readily signed on. Parishioners who knew one another only by name, who had, until then, exchanged only pleasant but perfunctory hellos on Sundays, were now working together to rebuild not just their beautiful building but the community they had taken for granted.

And, in their grief and loss they felt that first Sunday morning in their temporary quarters, they prayed and sang in a way few had ever experienced before.

In the new journey they had begun as a church, they had rediscovered the God within them.

The congregation had experienced an "epiphany" — the manifestation of the holy in their midst. The Gospel Epiphany is a story about seeking and finding the God within, the God in our midst. As the magi undertakes a long and arduous search for this mythical king by the light of the mysterious star (encountering, among other things, a murderous tyrant along the way), the suddenly churchless parish rediscovers, in their coming together to deal with the catastrophic loss of their church building, the Spirit of God within them that makes *them* the *real* church.

The story of the astrologers and the star of Bethlehem are unique to Matthew's Gospel. Note that Matthew does not call them kings, does not give their names, does not report where they came from — in fact, Matthew never even specifies the number of magi (because three gifts are presented to the Child, it has been a tradition since the fifth century to picture "*three* wise men"). In stripping away the romantic layers that have been added to the story, Matthew's point can be better understood.

Several Old Testament ideas and images are found in this story of *epiphany* (from the Greek word for *appearance* or *manifestation*). The star, for example, is reminiscent of Balaam's prophecy that "a star shall advance from Jacob" (Numbers 24: 17). Many of the details in Matthew's story about the child Jesus parallel the story of the child Moses and the Exodus.

Matthew's story also provides a preview of what is to come in his narrative. First, the reactions of the various parties to the birth of Jesus parallel the effects Jesus' teaching will have on those who hear it: Herod reacts with anger and hostility to the Jesus of the poor who comes to overturn the powerful and rich. The chief priests and scribes greet the news with haughty indifference toward the Jesus who comes to give new life and meaning to the rituals and laws of the scribes. But the magi — non-believers in the eyes of Israel — possess the humility of faith and the openness of mind and heart to seek and welcome the Jesus who will institute the Second Covenant between God and the New Israel.

Secondly, the gifts of the astrologers indicate the principal dimensions of Jesus' mission:

- **gold** is a gift fitting for a king, a ruler, one with power and authority;
- **frankincense** is a gift fitting for a priest, one who offers sacrifice (frankincense was an aromatic perfume sprinkled on the animals sacrificed in the Temple);
- **myrrh** is a fitting "gift" for someone who is to die (myrrh was used in ancient times for embalming the bodies of the dead before burial).

The magi's following of the star is a journey of faith, a constant search for meaning, for purpose, for the things of God; their search mirrors our own life-long search for the compassion, peace, justice and forgiveness that is *Emmanuel*. Epiphany is to embrace the light of the Christ that enables us to realize the presence of God in our midst — the God who is always present if not always apparent.

*C*hrist, the very light of God,
be the star we follow on our journey
to the dwelling place of God;
in your light, may we recognize all men and women
as our brothers and sisters under the loving providence
of the Father of all.
illuminate the roads and paths we travel,
that we may not stumble or turn back
from your way of peace, forgiveness and justice.

The Baptism of the Lord

On coming out of the water he saw the heavens being torn open and the Spirit, like a dove, descending upon him. A voice came from the heavens, "You are my beloved Son; with you I am well pleased."

Mark 1: 7–11

'The daughter of a whisper'

You first heard it as a child — the Voice. You wanted that extra candy bar or to escape the boundaries of the back yard or to slug your annoying little brother, but you heard that Voice saying, *Don't! You know what Mom said.* Now, you may not have paid any attention to the Voice. But you heard it. You know you did.

As you got older, the Voice spoke a little more critically. *That was dumb ... You really came off like a jerk ... What were you thinking?* But the Voice could also be encouraging and affirming: *Nice work ... You'll be glad you did that ... You didn't deserve that.* The Voice would prod, nudge or clobber. As you grew up, you understood that the Voice was right.

Eventually, you make friends with the Voice. You don't just listen to the Voice but you converse with the Voice. *"I'm not sure what to do here ... What was that all about? ... How can I make things better?"* And together, you and the Voice find a way to move on, to work it out, to put things back together.

In time, you begin to hear the Voice speaking more comforting and consoling words. *You are loved. You belong. You are mine.*

In the Jewish tradition, there is a name for that Voice: *bat cole,* which means literally, "the daughter of a sound." That "daughter of a sound," the smallest, thinnest of voices, is the Voice of God — God speaking to us in the events of our lives, in the people we love, in the characters and conundrums that challenge us.

In the story of his baptism at the Jordan, the *bat cole* is heard by Jesus: *You are my beloved Son, with you I am well pleased.* The fact that Mark begins his Gospel with the baptism of Jesus indicates the importance of this event to the early Christian community. In the "renting of the sky," the Spirit "descending on him like a dove" and the voice heard from the heavens, God "anoints" his Messiah (the word *Messiah* means "anointed") for the work he is about to do. In Mark's version of Jesus' baptism, it is unclear whether the "voice" was heard by others or by Jesus alone. The evangelist's point is that Jesus' Messiahship is affirmed by the Father in the waters of the Jordan.

We are the beloved of God; God claims us as his own. And unless and until we hear the voice from heaven claiming that we are cherished by a God who is "well-pleased" with us, we will never be able to truly cherish anyone or believe that we are their beloved as well. The voice of the Father — our Father — speaks to all of us in the sacrament of Baptism; the Spirit of God descends upon us, enabling us to give to others the love God joyfully gives to us.

May our hearts be attentive to that same Voice speaking to us in the course of the simple, undramatic every day of our lives — the Voice of God cajoling and nudging us to his dwelling place.

*I*n our baptism, O God,
you raised us out of the waters
into the life of your compassion and peace.
May your Spirit that descended upon us then
continue to transform us into prophets of your peace;
may your Voice continue to speak to our hearts,
directing us in the work of discipleship
and guiding us on the way
    to your eternal dwelling place.

LENT

Ash Wednesday

"Your Father who sees what is hidden will repay you."
Matthew 6: 1–6, 16–18

Even now, says the Lord, return to me with your whole heart ...
Joel 2: 12–18

We implore you, in Christ's name, be reconciled to God.
2 Corinthians 5: 20 – 6:2

Spring cleaning, Lenten planting

*T*oday we begin our annual Lenten pilgrimage with ashes. As our brothers and sisters in the faith have done since antiquity, we place ashes on our heads as powerful signs that we acknowledge our sinfulness and realize our mortality.

There are two particular properties of ashes that might add to our understanding this holy season and the Easter mystery we anticipate in the weeks ahead.

At one time, ashes were used to make soap. Ashes contain alkali, a chemical that is soluble in water and is a powerful cleaning agent. Let this Lent be the beginning of a time of cleaning and purification — a washing away of the grime of selfishness, hatred and mistrust in our lives, a spring cleaning of all of those things that draw our attention away from God and the things of God.

In some locales at this time of year, farmers burn the stubble of last year's crops still in the field; the remaining ashes are then plowed into the earth. The chemicals in the ashes serve as a powerful fertilizer for the new crops soon to be planted. Let this Lent, then, be a planting season for souls and spirits — a time for the word of God to take root in our lives, a growing season for our hearts and spirits to be transformed from barrenness to harvest, from despair to hope, from death to life.

Today, in a ritual dating back to the days of the prophets and kings of Israel, we place ashes on our heads — a powerful reminder that dust is exactly what we are.

And yet there is a certain sense of hope in these ashes. In ancient times, ashes were signs of repentance and mourning. Sinners seeking reconciliation with God and their communities covered their heads with ashes to express their sorrow for the wrong they had done and their resolve to transform their lives. To dust oneself in ashes was a sign of humility: the realization that God has raised us up from the ashes of the ground and that, in death, our bodies will again be reduced to ashes. The admonition articulated in our present rite expresses this understanding "Remember that you are dust and into dust you will return," from Genesis 3: 19 (other Scriptural references to the sign of ashes: Jeremiah 6: 26, Job 42: 3–6, Numbers 19: 9 and 19: 17, and Jonah 3:4–10).

The journey our spirits begin today, we know, ends not in ashes and dust but in life and hope. We know that we will encounter the cross along our Lenten road, but in its wood we will discover the first buds of eternity. The three readings on this Ash Wednesday speak of these themes of reconciliation and hope: In today's Gospel, from his Sermon on the Mount, Jesus calls his listeners to a deeper understanding of reconciliation and conversion through quiet, humble acts of prayer, fasting and almsgiving. The prophet Joel (Reading 1) summons Israel to a season of repentance that will transform individual hearts and reconcile their nation to the Lord of compassion and mercy. In his second letter to the Corinthians (Reading 2), Paul appeals for reconciliation among the members of the badly fractured church at Corinth, for a return to the one faith shared by the entire Church.

The challenge of these ashes is to bring forth from the ashes of our lives the forgiveness, mercy and justice of Christ. God invites us to be transformed from the dust of the earth into the life of God in whose image our souls beneath this dust are all cast.

*G*racious God,
may we begin our 40 days' Lenten springtime
by embracing the meaning of these ashes.
As we were once washed in the waters of baptism,
may the word of your Son clean us again of our sins
and purify us in hope and joy.
During these early spring days,
may your word take root within us,
that we may know the harvest
   of your mercy and compassion
in every season of every year.

The Spirit drove Jesus out into the desert, and he remained in the desert for 40 days, tempted by Satan.

Mark 1: 12–15

Beckoned by the desert

A traveler describes the sense of the sacred he experienced in the deserts of the American Southwest:

"The desert offers the comfort of permanence, the promise of continuity in a world of change ... [but it] is a vast and lonely landscape, with great distances separating the few locations that provide any protection and comfort. Intensified by stretches of unbroken vistas of land and sky, perspective is distorted. Roads are few, and those are no more than dirt trails, rutted and strewn with rocks, impassably muddy after a rain or packed as concrete by the bleaching sun. Even the best prepared may meet the unexpected, the freak storm, the slip or fall off a trail, the sudden strike of the surprised rattlesnake. In the final analysis, only the fool thinks he can rely on his strength and skill alone. In short, the desert escapes my control.

"For this reason my mind is drawn quietly, patiently, naturally toward someone outside myself on whom I can lean. In the desert I think not so much of causes as of the Cause, whatever or whoever holds all of this firm but fragile being in existence ... The desert escorts me out of myself, drawing me away from self-occupation, self absorption ... the desert is not conducive, immediately and directly, to producing 'inner peace' as are some other landscapes. Rather than turning inward, the experience of the desert is more about recognizing God's glory in the created world than about finding the divine spark within. The desert experience calls forth gratitude, thanksgiving and trust, not brooding introspection.

"We may, like Jesus, meet and be tempted by the enemy in the desert. We may, like the Baptist, be forced to dine on grasshoppers and wild honey, or, like Paul, discover our life's mission in a desert encounter with God's grace. One thing is certain, however: If we come to the desert, we will change."[1]

The Lenten season begins in the wilderness. Mark's brief account of Jesus' 40 days in the wilderness takes place immediately after Jesus' baptism. The same Spirit that "drove" Jesus into the desert drives us into our own deserts this Lent to change and be changed. In the uncompromising light of the desert landscape, the Spirit illuminates our consciences to see beyond ourselves to realize God's grace in our lives. "Driven by the Spirit," Jesus' going to the desert is an act of obedience to the Father. This is a time for contemplation and discernment regarding the tremendous task before him.

The word *Satan* comes from the Hebrew word for *adversary.* Satan serves as the adversary of God, advocating those values that contradict and oppose the love and mercy of God. Mark's portrait of Jesus in the desert is one of a Messiah coming to terms with the paradox of the human condition. As Jesus spent 40 days in the wilderness to discern what God was calling him to do with the next part of his life, the Spirit calls us to our own "wilderness experience" to confront the hard choices we must make in our lives — choices between the values of God and the far lesser things of the world that can isolate us, hurt others and diminish God's creation. Lent calls us away from business as usual (the real motivation behind giving up one's favorite confection or pastime) to decide, in the depths of our hearts where God speaks to each one of us, what it means to be a person of faith, what values we want our lives to stand for, what path we want our lives to take on our journey to God and Easter resurrection.

This Lent, walk with God in the desert of your heart; listen to God speaking to you away from the clamor of your busy days; realize his presence in your midst and discover new hope, new perspectives and new possibilities for Easter transformation.

*C*hrist of the desert,
journey with us on our own journeys
through the wilderness of doubt and fear;
be the light that guides us through the lonely deserts
where we hear you speaking to us
in the depths of our hearts,
where we see who we really are,
where we must choose the path we will walk
beyond the austerity of the desert
and into the bright morning of Easter.

Second Sunday of Lent

Peter said to Jesus, "Rabbi, it is good that we are here! Let us make three tents: one for you, one for Moses, and one for Elijah."

Mark 9: 2–10
[Roman lectionary]

The hermit's church

*M*any, many years ago, a hermit made his home in a small hut on the edge of town. The humble solitary was beloved by the townspeople for his kindness and compassion to all. He gave away the food he grew in his small garden to the poor, he spent countless hours caring for the sick, he offered shelter to travelers. The hermit made his small corner of the forest a sanctuary for the animals of the wood; he maintained the small stream near his hermitage as a source of clean, pure water for farmers and villagers.

After a long life of service and prayer, the old hermit died. The people of the village considered him a saint — *their* saint. So they decided to honor their saint with a beautiful church in which they would bury his remains.

The project began with the town elders hosting a great banquet for all the rich and well-to-do. Many of the guests gave vast sums of money to be used as memorials for the church. Plans were then drawn up for the building — a beautiful edifice of the finest stone and marble. Workers then began to clear the land where the old hermit's hut had stood. The stream had to be diverted for the construction.

After many months of construction, the beautiful church was completed. The archbishop dedicated the building in an elaborate, impressive liturgy. The bones of the saintly hermit, placed in an ornate casket, were solemnly interred in the crypt below the altar. And then a great festival was held to celebrate the new church.

People still come from miles around to see the beautiful church where the saint is buried. His garden that once fed the poor is a quiet courtyard locked within the cathedral's cloister. His hut that once welcomed the stranger, his stream that provided life to all, his sanctuary for all God's creatures are long gone and forgotten; in the shadows of the great church, the poor and sick struggle along — invisible, unrecognized, disregarded, scorned.

In Mark's story of the transfiguration, Peter does not know what to say or how to react to the incredible scene he has witnessed. All he can offer is the suggestion of erecting three "tents" or shrines to commemorate the event. But the transfigured Christ asks more of us than memorials of wood and stone, of brick and mortar: He seeks to be a living presence that illuminates human hearts and transforms human history. The Christ that Peter and his companions behold on the mountain calls us to become what Archbishop Desmond Tutu calls "agents of transfiguration": to enable his love within us to transform despair into hope, sadness into joy, anguish into healing, estrangement into community.

The use of the Greek word *transfiguration* indicates that what the disciples saw in Jesus on Mount Tabor was a divinity that shone from within him. In the event witnessed by Peter, James and John on the mountain, the promise of the first covenant (Moses the great law giver and Elijah the great prophet) converges with the fulfillment of the new covenant (Jesus the Messiah). As God revealed his presence to Israel in the form of a cloud as he often did in the Old Testament (for example, the column of cloud that led the Israelites in the desert during the Exodus), on the mountain of the transfiguration, God again speaks in the form of a cloud, claiming the transfigured Jesus as his own Son.

This Lenten season is a time for each of us to experience such a "transfiguration" within ourselves — that the life of God within us may shine forth in lives dedicated to compassion, justice and reconciliation. In the "transfigured" love of Christ the Messiah-Servant, we can "transfigure" despair into hope, sadness into joy, anguish into healing, estrangement into community.

May the light of love
   illuminate our hearts, O God,
that we may discover the sense
   of your divinity within ourselves.
May that sacredness enable us
to see beyond our own needs, wants and interests
so that we may we set about
to transfigure our lives and our world
in your compassion, justice and forgiveness.

Second Sunday of Lent

"If any want to become my followers, let them deny themselves and take up their cross and follow me."

Mark 8: 31–38
[Common lectionary]

Cross moves

A ten-year-old boy lost his left arm in a devastating auto accident. Once he had recovered, he began lessons in judo.

His teacher — his *sensei* — was an old Japanese master. The boy was doing very well. But he could not understand why, after three months of lessons, the master had taught him only one move.

"*Senei,*" the boy finally asked, "shouldn't I be learning more moves?"

"Yes, it is the only move you know — but it is the only move you'll ever need to know," the *sensei* replied.

Not quite understanding, but believing in his teacher, the boy continued training and mastering his move.

Several months later, the *sensei* took the boy to his first tournament. To his surprise, the student easily won his first two matches. The third match proved to be more difficult, but after some time, his opponent became impatient and charged; the boy deftly employed his one move and won the match. Still amazed at his success, the boy was now in the finals.

This time his opponent was bigger, stronger and more experienced. The boy appeared to be overmatched. Concerned that the boy might get hurt, the referee called a timeout. He was about to stop the match when the sensei intervened. "No, let them continue," the *sensei* said.

As the match continued, the boy's opponent made a critical mistake: he dropped his guard and the boy used his move to pin him. The boy won the match and the tournament.

On the way home, the boy and his teacher reviewed every move of every match. Then the boy finally summoned the courage to ask what was really on his mind.

"*Sensei*, how did I win the tournament with only one move?"

"You won for two reasons," the *sensei* answered. "First, you have almost mastered one of the most difficult moves in all of judo. And second, the only known defense for that move is for your opponent to grab your *left* arm."

Throughout his Gospel, Mark portrays a Jesus who is continually misunderstood by family and friends. Today's Gospel (in the common lectionary) is a case-in-point. Jesus tells his disciples that his ministry will end in suffering and death in Jerusalem. Peter takes Jesus aside and admonishes him for speaking such a gruesome message. Jesus reacts with surprising sharpness to Peter's rebuke. The hard reality for Peter and his companions (including us) to accept is that the cross is central to Jesus' Messiahship — and must be a part of every follower's acceptance of Jesus' call to discipleship. To be part of the new life of Christ's resurrection in the life to come requires dying to our own needs and wants in the present.

We all have crosses to bear. We tend to think of our particular cross as a burden, something — or someone — that demands so much of our time and energy. We consider whatever weighs us down, causes us pain or anguish, traps us in lives of desperation and despair as the "crosses" we have to bear. We dream of the day when we can lay our crosses aside, never to pick them up again.

But, as the young judo warrior-in-training discovers, often our heaviest cross can be our greatest strength. Many of our crosses are opportunities to be sources of hope, of joy, of discovery, of healing, of life for ourselves and others. Christ now challenges us to transform those crosses into vehicles of resurrection. With the crosses he lays on our shoulders, God animates our hearts with his grace in the form of the strength to cope, the ability to listen and console, the faculty to lead and lift up. These crosses, when taken up in the same spirit of humble compassion with which Jesus took up his, are the first light of Easter dawn.

*C*hrist Jesus, give us the grace and courage
to take up the crosses laid upon our shoulders.
Help us to "crucify" our own narrow interests
and self-centered wants
so that we may bring to our families and communities
the joy and hope of Easter.

Jesus made a whip out of cords and drove the money changers out of the temple area and spilled the coins of the money changers and overturned their tables. "Take these out of here, and stop making my Father's house a marketplace."

John 2: 13–25

Spring cleaning

He has had this quirk going back to college: the need to clean, even under pressure. The night before an exam or facing the deadline to complete a major paper, he'd dive into it: cleaning the drawers of his desk and bureau, straightening out his closet, doing laundry, ironing shirts, slacks and handkerchiefs, vacuuming the rugs, organizing the books on his shelves — even dusting the furniture. And throwing out stuff — several trips would be made to the incinerator before he was done. Only after everything was clean and in order would he be ready to tackle the notes for his biology exam or start drafting his economics paper. To this day, before any major project or task, whether cooking dinner or planning a business presentation, everything has to be in its place.

Many of us are driven to spring cleaning with the same attitude. Serious spring cleaning demands a commitment of mental as well as physical energy, a resolve to bring order to our lives and to remove the unnecessary, the distracting and the useless that have accumulated in our lives over the winter. The first warm breeze compels us to wash away the mud season grime that has settled on our windows and walls and to open our dwellings to let in the clean, fresh air of a new spring. There is something liberating in raking up the debris that winter has settled among the bushes and in the gutters; there is a sense of victory in sweeping up the salt and sand from our driveways and sidewalks from the winter past, and (especially) in getting the car washed after weeks of mud, salt and dirt.

When the tasks are completed, there's a sense of newness that not only freshens our homes but invigorates our spirits, as well.

Our late winter yearning for newness, for cleansing, for fresh air, puts Jesus' angry expulsion of the merchants from the temple into perspective. Christ comes to bring a new spirit to humankind, to illuminate a springtime of hope to a people who have lived too long in a winter of alienation and despair. For the evangelist John, today's Gospel is a metaphor of that newness. Whereas the Synoptic Gospels place Jesus' cleansing of the temple immediately after his Palm Sunday entrance into Jerusalem, John places the event early in his Gospel, following Jesus' first sign at Cana. While the Synoptics recount only one climactic journey to Jerusalem, the Jesus of John's Gospel makes several trips to the holy city.

Pilgrims to the temple were expected to make a donation for the upkeep and expenses of the edifice. Because Roman currency was considered "unclean," Jewish visitors had to change their money into Jewish currency in order to make their temple gift. Moneychangers, whose tables lined the outer courts of the temple, charged exorbitant fees for their service. Visiting worshipers who wished to have a sacrifice offered on the temple altar would typically pay 15 to 20 times the market rate for animals purchased inside the temple. Vendors could count on the cooperation of the official temple "inspectors" who, as a matter of course, would reject as "unclean" or "imperfect" animals brought in from outside the temple.

Jesus' angry toppling of the vendors' booths and tables is a condemnation of the injustice and exploitation of the faithful in the name of God. So empty and meaningless has their worship become that God will establish a new "temple" in the resurrected body of the Christ.

Of course, the leaders and people do not appreciate the deeper meaning of Jesus' words, nor did the people who witnessed his miracles understand the true nature of his Messianic mission.

John's closing observations in this reading point to the fact that the full meaning of many of Jesus' words and acts were understood only later, in the light of his resurrection.

Lent (which comes from the old English word for *springtime*) is the time for a "spring cleaning" of our spirits and souls — for driving out of our lives the useless, the meaningless, the destructive. Our late winter yearning for the newness, freshness, warmth and light of spring mirrors Jesus' angry expulsion of the merchants from the temple. Christ comes to bring newness to humankind, to bring a springtime of hope to a people who have lived too long in a winter of alienation and despair.

In the temple precincts of our lives are "money changers" and connivers — fear, ambition, addictions, selfishness, prejudice — that distort the meaning of our lives and debase our relationships with God and with one another. Lent is a time to invite the "angry" Jesus of today's Gospel into our lives to drive out those things that make our lives less than what God created them to be.

May we prepare for the Easter festival by driving out the unnecessary and the useless from our lives, by raising our spirits through a "spring cleaning" of those things that clutter and "muddy" our relationships with God and with one another.

*C*ome, Lord of Easter newness,
and cleanse away the dirt of sin
and the mud of hopelessness
and restore the temples of our hearts
to fitting dwelling places for you.
Illuminate our spirits with the light of your Word
that every moment of our lives may give you praise
by our works of compassion and charity.

Fourth Sunday of Lent

[Jesus said to Nicodemus:] "God did not send the Son into the world to condemn the world, but in order that the world might be saved through him ... "

John 3: 14–21

After-hours prayer

*L*ate in the afternoon, a teenager sneaks into a back pew. He drops his backpack, unplugs his i-Pod, and stuffs his basketball behind the kneeler. His aloofness and sullenness mask his feelings of being overwhelmed by living in that strange land between childhood and adulthood, trying to meet the expectations of teachers to be a scholar, his coaches to be champion, and his classmates to be cool. In the quiet darkness, he sits and prays simply, "Lord, it's me, Joe ... "

In another part of the church, an exhausted businessman sinks into a seat. It has been a horrible day — he had to let five people go in his small agency. He had no choice: business is drying up. He did everything he could to keep them on; he offered severance pay and extended benefits; still, he feels like the worst person who ever lived. In the nightmare he is struggling through, he prays, "God, help me keep it together."

And in front of the statue of the Mother of God, a woman sits fingering her rosary. The *Aves* fall silently from her lips — but her thoughts are elsewhere: another confrontation with her daughter, the illness of her mother, the growing distance between her and her husband. She stops her beads, sinks to the floor and cries, "Lord, I'm not sure I can go on."

Like Nicodemus, we find ourselves coming to Jesus in the middle of our darkest nights, seeking hope and consolation, direction and comfort. Jesus' meeting with Nicodemus is one of the most hopeful and reassuring episodes in the Gospels.

Nicodemus is a Pharisee, a member of the ruling Sanhedrin. Like so many others who heard Jesus, he is fascinated by this worker of wonders. He arranges to meet Jesus at night, so as not to attract undue attention. In their meeting, Jesus tries to make Nicodemus understand the mission of the Messiah in a new light: It is not Israel's strict adherence to the ancient Law but the love of God that is the vehicle of salvation. Yahweh is not the God of condemnation and destruction but the God of forgiveness, mercy and reconciliation. God is motivated by a love so great that he gives the world his only Son, not to destroy but to transform the world. Redemption begins with God; reconciliation and healing are God's work, filled with possibilities that are as limitless as they are undeserved. God's Messiah is the "light" in which humankind sees the great love and mercy of God in their midst.

Contrary to Nicodemus and Judaism's expectation of a powerful, triumphant Messiah who will restore Israel's political fortunes, the real Messiah will suffer and die in order to conquer death and restore life. Jesus invokes the image of Numbers 21: 4–9: As Yahweh directs, Moses lifts up the image of a serpent on a pole to heal those who suffer from a deadly plague caused by the bite of serpents. The crucified Messiah, too, will be "lifted up" to bring healing and wholeness to this hurting world.

In his questioning and confusion, his fears and doubts, Nicodemus is welcomed by Jesus with understanding and compassion. In the Gospels, Jesus reveals a God of life and restoration, a God who seeks not our punishment or humiliation but our healing and reconciliation with Him and with one another. Too often, we approach faith as a series of "thou shalt nots" — religion is equated with guilt, spirituality with that nagging little conscience in the depths of our souls that serves as a safety valve to stop us from becoming the wicked people we know we're capable of becoming. Jesus challenges such a limited concept of faith: God is not a cosmic tyrant that revels in seeing us suffer; God has revealed himself as the loving Father of a perfect creation that has made itself imperfect in so many ways through sin.

Despite our rejection of the ways of God, our demeaning of the values of God, God continues to call us and seek us out. God loves his creation too much to write it off or condemn it; instead, God raises up his Son as a new light to illuminate our hearts, to make us see things as God sees them, to share God's hope for humanity's redemption.

O God, Author of love and source of compassion,
may we embrace the perspective of faith
    and attitude of hope
your Son revealed to Nicodemus.
With a sense of gratitude,
may we praise you as the Source of life
    and all that is good;
with humble joy,
may we embrace and be embraced
by your Spirit of compassion and forgiveness.
By your grace, help us to transform our darkest nights
into the morning light of hope;
by your wisdom, help us to transfigure
    our Good Friday despair into Easter joy;
by your compassion, heal our broken spirits
into hearts made whole.

Fifth Sunday of Lent

"Unless a grain of wheat falls to the ground and dies, it remains just a single grain; but if it dies, it bears much fruit."

John 12: 20–33

Breast cancer husband

*B*y his own admission, he didn't handle the news very well.

"Ew-w-w, that doesn't sound good" was all he could say when his wife called him from the doctor's office and told him that she might have breast cancer. They talked for just a few minutes, mainly about logistics (what to say to their two teenage daughters, when to set up a meeting with a surgeon). And hey, the doctor could be wrong, right? And then he said something like, "I'll be home at the usual time."

Not good. What was I thinking? he would ask himself later.

But despite the bad start, this husband discovered that there was a lot he could do for his wife.

First, he learned the importance of just being a good listener. He gave her a safe place to vent her anger and talk about her fears. The best thing he could say — and he said it often: "No matter what happens, you know I'm going to be here."

At first, he thought his job was to choose the best doctor he could find for his wife. But he soon understood that *she* had to choose a surgeon who made her feel confident and a course of treatment that made sense both to the doctor and to her. But he didn't sit idly by — he took on the frustrating fights with the HMO and served as her sounding board.

He learned the importance of just being there with her and holding her hand during appointments and conferences. He helped her formulate a list of questions prior to meeting with her doctor and he'd bring the list to the appointment. He made notes during those meetings, as well. If he couldn't be Mr. Fix-it, then he could be the Reminder Guy.

He managed to find the funny, reassuring, loving thing to say that made the pain and embarrassment of each step of her treatment bearable.

Ten months later, she finished radiation and the family settled into what they call the "new normal" in which they are acutely aware of the fragile nature of life. They've fallen back into many of their old ways and habits: slaving away at the same stressful jobs and grappling with the task of raising their two beautiful daughters. But things are different. He's different. He hopes she knows that, despite his dismal start as a breast cancer husband, she can count on him to be by her side.

And when he says "I love you," he's not just mouthing a cliché. [2]

The grain of wheat in today's Gospel is an important lesson about love: that the risk of being hurt, of being broken, of losing some part of ourselves, is the price of love.

Today's Gospel is a pivotal moment in John's narrative. Jesus' words about the "coming" of his "hour" mark the end of John's "Book of Signs" and prefaces "The Book of Glory" — the passion, death and resurrection of Jesus. The Passover is about to begin; many Jews (including some Greek Jews) have arrived in Jerusalem for the festival. Meanwhile, Jesus' conflict with the Jewish establishment has reached the crisis stage. The mechanics that will lead to Jesus' death are now in motion. Jesus obediently accepts his fate and is prepared for the outcome.

Jesus compares his "glorification" to a grain of wheat that is buried and dies to itself in order to produce new life. The sacrifice and harvest of the grain of wheat are the fate and glory of anyone who would be Jesus' disciple. The "voice" heard from the sky expresses the unity of Jesus' purpose and God's will.

To become the people God calls us to be begins by our "dying" to our doubts and fears, "dying" to our self-centered wants and needs, "dying" to our immaturity and prejudices. That is the challenge of the grain of wheat: only by loving is love returned, only by reaching out do we learn and grow, only by giving to others do we receive, only by dying do we rise to new life.

The Gospel of the grain of wheat is Christ's assurance to us of the great things we can do and the powerful miracles we can work in letting go of our prejudices, fears and ambitions in order to imitate the compassion and love of the crucified Jesus, the Servant Redeemer. As this husband learns, in our love and faithfulness to spouse and family and friends, we find within ourselves the potential bounty of the Gospel wheat: in our willingness to "die" to our fears, to put aside our own needs and wants, to let our lives be pulled apart, we discover love that can only be of God.

*C*hrist our Redeemer,
may we embrace the faith of the grain of wheat:
that we may willingly die
to our own wants, needs and fears
in order to experience the life of your resurrection
in our families, homes, schools and communities.
May we take up own our crosses
in your spirit of selflessness and compassion,
that we may transform our lives
    and the lives of those around us
in the complete joy of Easter.

Sunday of the Lord's Passion: Palm Sunday

The Blessing and Procession of Palms

Many people spread their cloaks on the road, and others spread leafy branches that they had cut from the fields. Those preceding him as well as those following kept crying out: "Hosanna! Blessed is he who comes in the name of the Lord!"

Mark 11: 1–10

Jesus found an ass and sat upon it, as it is written: *Fear no more, O daughter Zion; see, your king comes, seated upon an ass's colt.*

John 12: 12–16

Of faded branches and last hosannas

We begin our Holy Week observance on Palm Sunday with branches of palm — rich and green, soft and pliant, yet hearty and strong. They are long-awaited reminders that spring is (almost) here.

These branches we hold are much like our faith — not what our faith *should* be but what our faith often *is*. After the *Hosannas* are sung this weekend, we will tuck these palms away near a crucifix or icon. By Sunday evening they will become brittle and dry and gnarled and largely forgotten — until sometime next winter when we stick them in a bag and bring them to church to be burned and the residue used to smudge crosses on our heads next Ash Wednesday. Once these palms have been safely tucked away until next Lent, it's business as usual: we return to our *Hosanna*-less lives of struggle and pain and brokenness.

These palms are a parable of our faith, our belief in this Jesus, our embracing of his Gospel. On holy days, at milestone celebrations of the sacraments, our faith is as rich and green as these palms are today. But when our faith starts to pull at our consciences, when we hear Jesus pointing us to a course of action outside our comfort zone, when the pursuit of our dreams demand cutting a few moral and ethical corners, then our faith becomes as brittle and dry and gnarled and forgotten as these palms will be tomorrow.

In Gospel times, to wave palm branches was considered a political statement, not a religious act. The palm was the symbol of Roman victory: to take up palm branches was to have conquered your enemy. In waving palm branches to welcome Jesus, the crowds were in effect welcoming Jesus not as the Messiah but as their nation's king; this was a gesture of defiance against their Roman rulers and occupiers. Their hope was that this renowned rabbi and wonder-worker would save them from the tyranny of the Roman establishment and restore their land to nationhood and economic and political power.

But the palm-wavers would be horribly disappointed before the week was over.

In the light of the Gospel, these palms are not symbols of triumph but of human folly, the illusion of what passes for victory and success in the world. Christ enters the Jerusalems of our lives not to restore nations but to reclaim hearts, not to realize ambitions but to raise up spirits. The palms we wave are not signs of the triumph of a political king but the suffering of the God's Messiah, whose final victory over death transcends the vagaries of our materialistic dreams and the impermanence of our brief time on earth.

These palms confront us with what our baptisms into the death and resurrection of Jesus demand of us. As we welcome the Christ of victory this Sunday, may we be just as welcoming of the Christ of suffering. As we embrace the Gospel of the Jesus of love, may we also embrace the Jesus of justice, of humility, of selflessness. As we try to imitate Jesus' compassion, may we also be willing to imitate his limitless reconciliation and unconditional forgiveness. May these palms — whether green or cracked, pliant or gnarled — remind us every day in every season of Christ's promise that despite the many Good Fridays of our lives, Easter morning will always dawn.

Mark's account of Jesus' entry into Jerusalem is the most subdued version of the event in the Gospels. The donkey plays a central role in the Mark's story — Mark relates with surprising detail how the disciples found the donkey colt as Jesus told them. In his short account of Jesus' entry into Jerusalem, John makes specific reference to Zechariah's prophecy (Zechariah 9: 9) that the Messiah-king will enter the city seated on "a donkey's colt." It was the custom for pilgrims to enter Jerusalem on foot. Only great kings and rulers would "ride" into the city — and usually on great steeds and horses. Jesus, the King of the new Jerusalem, chooses to ride into the city — but not on a majestic stallion but on the back of a young beast of burden. By being led through the city on the back of a lowly, servile donkey, Jesus comes as a King whose rule is not about being served but giving generous and selfless service to others; his kingdom is not built on might but on compassion. The little donkey Jesus mounts mirrors how the prophet Zechariah foretold this scene five centuries before: "Rejoice greatly, O daughter Zion! Shout aloud, O daughter Jerusalem! See, your king comes to you, triumphant and victorious is he, humble and riding on a donkey … "

The Reading of the Passion

At three o'clock, Jesus cried out in a loud voice, "Eloi, Eloi, lema sabacthani?" which is translated, "My God, my God, why have you forsaken me?"

Mark 14: 1 – 15: 47

The 'crucifiers'

The governor knew that the prisoner dragged before him was innocent, the victim of one of the greatest smear campaigns ever perpetrated. But justice was not the governor's concern. Keeping things under control for his Roman masters — in order to hold on to his comfortable position — was all that mattered. And what of it if a nobody carpenter from some backwater is crushed in the process? *Jesus is crucified on the cross of Pilate's cowardice.*

The high priest was a revered figure among the Jews. He was a devout and sincerely religious man. He saw it as his duty to protect his faith from this anarchist who questioned the rituals and challenged the teachings the high priest held sacred. As many have done throughout history, he and his Sanhedrin put creed before mercy and institution before community — with disastrous results. *Jesus is crucified on the cross of the high priest's rigid, dehumanizing, intolerant belief that the high priest alone possessed the "truth."*

He didn't really do it for the money. He was cutting his losses. He had seen promise in this young rabbi. *He might be the one,* he thought at the beginning. *This could be the long-awaited Messiah who would restore our nation to power.* But it became clear that they did not share the same vision of the "reign" of God: While he envisioned the "kingdom" as the restoration of his people's political and economic power, the rabbi kept talking about a kingdom of spirit, a kingdom of peace and justice, a kingdom built on selfless generosity and humble service to the poor and forgotten. He couldn't wait any longer. Time to move on. Take the money and find another Messiah. *Jesus is crucified on the cross of Judas' impatient, singular need for results.*

The officers and soldiers who arrested Jesus? *Just doing our jobs.*

The crowds who watched him stumble through the streets under the crossbeam strapped to his shoulders? *Too bad. He did alot of good things for people. But if you're gonna take on the big guys, you're gonna get hurt.*

Those who pass by the dying Jesus hanging on the tree? *Please, we don't want to get involved. It's not our business.*

Jesus is crucified on the cross — a cross made of cowardice, self-righteousness, power, expediency, fear and silence.

On this Passion Sunday, we are confronted with the death of Jesus on the cross. Jesus is crucified not because of wild viciousness or sadistic brutality or naked hate but because of the more "civilized" vices of self-interest, bigotry, indifference, fear and half-truths — vices we all share, the very vices which crucify human beings today. The cross symbolizes the very worst we fail to see in ourselves, that part of us we deftly justify in order to rationalize the crucifixions we execute.

In his account of the Passion, Mark portrays the anguish of Jesus who has been totally abandoned by friends and disciples. There is no one to defend him, to support him, to speak for him. Jesus endures such a cruel and unjust death alone. Mark's Jesus is resigned to his fate. He makes no response to Judas when he betrays him or to Pilate during his interrogation (and Pilate makes no effort to save him, as the procurator does in the other three Gospels). Fully aware of the consequences, Jesus responds to the chief priest's questioning that he is the long-awaited Christ. Mark pointedly portrays the utter failure of the disciples to provide any assistance or support to Jesus or to even understand what is happening. The "last" disciple who flees naked into the night when Jesus is arrested is a powerful symbol in Mark's Gospel of the disciples who left family and friends behind to follow Jesus now leave everything behind to get away from him.

Yet, amid the darkness, a light glimmers: The prophecy of a new temple "not made by human hands" is fulfilled in the shreds of the temple curtain; a pagan centurion confesses his new-found realization that this crucified Jesus is indeed the "Son of God"; and a member of the Sanhedrin, Joseph of Arimathea, is embolden to break with his fellow councilors and request of Pilate the body of Jesus. The Passion of Jesus should be a reason for hope and a moment of grace for all of us as we seek the reign of God in our own lives — however lonely and painful our search may be.

As we journey with Jesus this Holy Week, may we realize the crosses we have sanctioned and how we can transform them into experiences of resurrection by taking them up in the spirit of Jesus' humble and selfless compassion.

*C*hrist our Redeemer,
may we not only remember
your passion, death and resurrection this Holy Week,
but may we enter, heart and soul,
into your passion, death and resurrection.
May the example of your selfless compassion

guide out faltering steps
as we struggle to follow you
    from Jerusalem to the upper room,
    from agony to trial,
    from crucifixion to burial.
May we empty ourselves of our own hurts and wants
in order to become lights of your mercy
and consolation for others;
may we take up our crosses as you took up yours
in the certain hope that our experiences of crucifixion
    for the sake of justice and integrity
will be transformed into the vindication of Easter.

THE EASTER
TRIDUUM

Holy Thursday

"If I, the master and teacher, have washed your feet, you ought to wash one another's feet."

John 13: 1–15

This day shall be a memorial feast for you, which all your generations shall celebrate with pilgrimage to the LORD, as a perpetual institution.

Exodus 12: 1–8, 11–14

"This is my body that is for you. Do this in remembrance of me."

1 Corinthians 11: 23–26

Remembering

A family learned the dreaded diagnosis: their mother was suffering the onset of Alzheimer's Disease. Over the next few months, her memories — already slowly slipping away — would fade to black all together. Her daughter-in-law reflects on the preciousness of memories that she and her husband, John, began to realize as his mother's memory began to slip away.

"Life is about moments — the blessed, the tragic, the sidesplitting, the poignant. Our lives are framed by them, and each one of us has the assemblage of memories that could be edited together, set to music, and watched like a movie ... Memories comfort us. They make us who we are. Without a connection to who we were, we'd feel lost, which must be exactly how [my mother-in-law] feels. We want her so badly to remember us, and often she does, but we know we won't always be that lucky ...

"John once told me, 'I want to make memories with you.' It was a funny thing for a guy to say, but I know what he meant. He wanted me in his life, and he wanted to remember all of it.

"Memories are a privilege — every day we get to choose whether we want to remember something … and when those moments are slipping away, it reminds you how much there is to lose.

"We started keeping a memory book, John and I. It's a cloth book that we keep on our bedside table where we'll record a note about a fun day we had or a silly moment. Maybe it's human not to write the sad stuff. But it's our way of keeping a record. Now, even if one of us forgets, there will always be those voices, our voices, on the page speaking to us."[1]

Memories are very precious things. Those of us who have suffered with a loved one afflicted with any form of dementia know all too well how fragile our ability to remember.

Tonight is about reliving a memory: the memory of Jesus, the Christ, who begins this night, for our sakes, his great Passover from death to life. At this table, in the cenacle of our own church, the memory of Jesus becomes a living reality. The rabbi Jesus speaks to us again in the pages of the Gospel book, in the basin, pitcher and towel, in the Eucharistic bread and wine.

Jesus, who revealed the wonders of God in stories about mustard seeds, fishing nets and ungrateful children, on this last night of his life — as we know life — leaves his small band of disciples his most beautiful parable: *As I have washed your feet like a slave, so you must wash the feet of each other and serve one another. As I have loved you without limit or condition, so you must love one another without limit or condition. As I am about to suffer and die for you, so you must suffer and, if necessary, die for one another.* Tonight's parable is so simple, but its lesson is so central to what being a real disciple of Christ is all about. When inspired by the love of Christ, the smallest act of service done for another takes on extraordinary dimensions.

Whenever we imitate Jesus' compassion and humility in putting aside our robes, bending down and "washing the feet" of another, the memory of Jesus' compassion lives again. Whenever we gather at this table to break and bless the bread and cup and share it, we experience again the selfless compassion of Jesus.

This night challenges us to make the memory of Jesus' compassionate healing and humble love for all humanity live again

The Easter Triduum

in our taking on the *mandatum* of being footwashers to one another, of becoming the community of the Eucharist Christ has envisioned us to become.

*G*racious Father,
tonight we remember the beginning
   of Jesus' "Passover."
Help us to be faithful to his memory —
to remember his life and love among us:
As he washed the feet of his disciples,
may we humbly and joyfully wash the feet
   of one another
and allow others to wash our feet
   in acts of kindness and forgiveness.
As we receive this night the bread and wine
   of the Eucharist,
may we become Christ's body and blood
for our broken, hurting world;
may we become joyful and generous footwashers
to all your children who come to this table with us.
Let the memory of his life among us
be a light for our own lives;
let his emptying himself for our sakes
inspire us to become servants for one another;
let his resurrection be our hope
   of the ultimate victory of love over all.

Good Friday

So they took Jesus and, carrying the cross himself, he went out to what is called the Place of the Skull, in Hebrew, Golgotha. There they crucified him, with two others, one on either side, Jesus in the middle.

John 18: 1 — 19: 42

Sacred tree

*I*n a remote village in Tanzania stands a giant baobab tree. The old tree has been completely hollowed out by the passing of the centuries. Its roots reach deep down into the African earth. Its branches — more than 75 feet in length — stretch out to embrace the deep blue equatorial sky. The hollow trunk is more than 60 feet in diameter.

The old tree is sacred to the village. It is their gathering place: each evening, the village shaman recounts the sacred stories of their history; it is the place where the community celebrates, with dancing and drums, the milestones of birth and marriage and death, and offers prayers of thanksgiving for the good fortunes of the harvest.

The sacred baobab is also the community's "birthing tree." When a pregnant woman comes to term, she enters the hollow sanctuary of the baobab where she gives birth to her child. The sacred tree offers mother and child shelter from the heat and rain, the beauty of its large sweet-smelling flowers, and the nourishment of its seeds and fruit.

Every child in the village first sees the light of day within the shelter of the old tree.

Today, our community gathers at our sacred tree: the cross of Good Friday. We hear the story again of how a loving God gave himself up for us on this tree; like the ancient African baobab, we are reborn within the embrace of the wood of the cross. In and through this sacred tree, we experience the light of the resurrection. This holy tree is hope for our defeated beings, grace for our battered souls, sustenance for our starving spirits. In the cross of Christ, we realize the possibilities for healing, for forgiveness, for reconciliation, for transformation, for re-creation.

The cross repulses us and shames us, confronting us with death and humiliation, with the injustice and betrayal of which we are all capable. But the cross is also the tree of life through which we are reborn. The tree of defeat becomes the tree of victory; where life was lost, there life will be restored. The tree of Good Friday will blossom anew, bringing life, not death; bringing light that shatters centuries of darkness; bringing Paradise, not destruction. As Jesus' cross becomes a means of transforming death into life, we are called on this Good Friday to use the crosses that we shoulder in our lives as vehicles for "resurrection" in the Jerusalems and Golgothas of our own time and place.

May the branches of this tree be a place of welcome and peace for all of us; may the Holy One who gave his life on this tree be a constant source of life and love for all who come to stand in its shadow.

*T*oday we stand at the foot of your cross, O Christ.
By this sacred tree may we be re-born
in your compassion and forgiveness;
may it always be a living sign for us
of what you have called us to be;
may it be the perfect symbol for us
of how to live the lives our baptisms compel us to live.
May your Good Friday cross be our gathering place
    as your people:
your witnesses of your resurrection
and lights of your continued presence in our midst.

The Easter Vigil

"Do not be amazed! You seek Jesus of Nazareth, the crucified.
He has been raised; he is not here. Behold the place where they
laid him."

Mark 16: 1–7

The last verse

*T*here is one more verse to Mark's story of Jesus' resurrection, a verse that is not included in tonight's lectionary selection:

"[The women] went out and fled from the tomb, seized with trembling and bewilderment. They said nothing to anyone, *for they were afraid.*" [Emphasis added.]

Mark's Gospel (the oldest of the four canonical Gospel texts) continues for another eleven verses, with brief stories of the Risen Jesus appearing to Mary Magdalene and to the Eleven and of the Ascension — but Biblical scholars have concluded that these were added to Mark's original in the first and second centuries by Christians wanting to "complete" Mark's account with post-Resurrection stories from the early Church's rich oral tradition. The writing style and themes of these added verses are unlike anything else in Mark's Gospel.

Succeeding generations of Christians must have found it hard to live with the cryptic, unsatisfying — even disturbing — "nonending." But scholars are convinced that Mark himself ended his text abruptly with the words "they were afraid": Jesus has been raised from the dead, and the compassionate women who risk coming to the tomb early on Sunday morning to complete the work of burial hear the angel's news and run in terror.

The end.

But isn't that our own first reaction to the news of Jesus' resurrection, as well? The truth is that Easter scares us. We can handle the birth of a child at Christmas with great joy — but the rebirth of the crucified Jesus is terrifying. We can bury Jesus whose life personified the very compassion and forgiveness of God — but the rising of that life from the grave forces us to the uncomfortable, unnerving task of confronting the values and beliefs of our own lives.

In Mark's Good Friday account, Jesus was buried quickly because sundown was approaching and the Sabbath was about to begin. Mary Magdalene, Mary the mother of James and Salome return to the tomb Sunday morning to come to complete the ritual anointings that had to be omitted two nights before. The problem of the rock at the entrance of the tomb was no small obstacle: Tombs in Gospel times were large caves in which several bodies could be laid. The entrance to these caves would then be closed off with a large, flat, round stone fitted into a track dug into the ground. But the three faithful women will not be deterred by a stone. They were focused on their task: to properly and compassionately complete the burial of their slain friend and teacher.

They are not prepared for what they find.

A "young man" proclaims to the terrified women in Mark's Easter Gospel that all that God has promised and all that Jesus taught has been fulfilled. The young man instructs the three women to go and tell the disciples "and Peter" what has happened. Remember that throughout his Gospel, Mark has made a point of the disciples' constant failure to understand and grasp the meanings of the Servant-Messiah's words and actions. Mark's singling out of Peter indicates the new life of forgiveness and reconciliation that Peter — who denied the condemned Jesus three days before — will receive from the Risen Christ.

But, as Mark writes in what scholars agree is the final line of his Gospel (verse 8), they were too afraid to say anything to anyone.

Mark calls us to complete the Gospel ourselves; the evangelist challenges us to confront our own fears and questions regarding the meaning of this unfathomable act of God. In raising his Son from the dead, God vindicates the Gospel of forgiveness, compassion and justice revealed by his Christ — a Gospel that an unholy conspiracy sought to bury, a Gospel that we often prefer to entomb in shrines and beautifully crafted but closed Bibles. The Resurrection is God's pushing us to the unknown and demanding Galilees of the poor, the marginalized, the lost, the despised; the Easter Christ yanks us out of the safe "tombs" we have dug for ourselves to keep the difficult and different, to protect ourselves in our self-centered and self-created purgatories.

And that is terrifying.

*F*ather, tonight we celebrate the empty tomb
    of your Son —
your ultimate promise of hope, of life, of love
    to humanity.
May the joy of this night give us the grace and hope
to abandon the tombs we create for ourselves
and bring the resurrection into this life of ours;
to renew and re-create our world in the light
    of the Risen Christ;
to proclaim in every moment of our lives
the Gospel of the Holy One, Christ Jesus
who has died, who has risen, and who comes again!

EASTER

Easter Sunday

On the first day of the week, Mary of Magdala came to the tomb early in the morning, while it was still dark, and saw the stone removed from the tomb. So she ran and went to Simon Peter and to the other disciple whom Jesus loved, and told them "They have taken the Lord from the tomb, and we don't know where they put him."

John 20: 1–9

'Let him easter in us'

On December 8, 1875, the German ship *Deutschland* sank in the North Sea, off the English coast. Among the 157 passengers who perished were five Franciscan sisters traveling to Missouri to take up new teaching missions. The young nuns sacrificed their own lives so that others might be rescued. According to one account, the sisters remained below deck as the ship sank. As the water rose around them, they clasped hands and were heard praying, "O Christ, O Christ, come quickly!"

The Jesuit poet Gerard Manley Hopkins was profoundly moved by the story and wrote a poem about the tragedy, *The Wreck of the Deutschland,* which he dedicated to the five Franciscans. He saw in their deaths a parallel to the suffering of Christ. Hopkins concludes the poem with this line:

Let him easter in us, be a dayspring to the dimness of us ...

As used here, the word "easter" is a nautical term: to steer a craft toward the east, into the light.

Let him easter in us.

Easter as a *verb* — not just the name of this great festival we begin today, not just the mystery of God's unfathomable redemptive love that the Gospel can barely articulate, but Easter as something we *think,* something we *feel,* something we do.

Let him easter in us that we may live our lives in the light of his compassion and peace, his justice and forgiveness.

Let him easter in us that we may be a humble servant like him, a healer like him, a teacher like him, a footwasher like him.

Let him easter in us that we may bear our crosses for one another as he bore his cross for us.

Let him easter in us that we may, at the end of our voyage, "easter" in him.

Easter as a verb, as something renewing and re-creating and transforming, is mirrored in John's account of Easter morning. As he does throughout his Gospel, John describes the actual "sign" or miracle of divine intervention directly, simply and unembellished. John's greater interest is the reaction of the witnesses and how they are changed by the act. In John's resurrection story, there are no earthquakes or angels (they appear later). The tomb is empty, the burial shroud and wrappings are on the ground, and the cloth that covered the face of Jesus rolled up.

Mary of Magdala (the one common thread in all four Gospel accounts) goes to the tomb alone. It was believed that the spirit of the deceased hovered around the tomb for three days after burial; Mary was therefore following the Jewish custom of visiting the tomb during this three-day period. Discovering that the stone has been moved away, Mary Magdalene runs to tell Peter and the others. Peter and the "other disciple" race to get there and look inside.

Note the different reactions of the three: Mary fears that someone has "taken" Jesus' body; Peter does not know what to make of the news; but the "other" disciple — the model of faithful discernment in John's Gospel — immediately understands what has taken place. So great are the disciple's love and depth of faith that all of the strange remarks and dark references of Jesus now become clear to him.

Today we stand, with Mary, Peter and the "other" disciple, at the entrance of the empty tomb; with them, we wonder what this "eastering" means. The Christ who challenged us to love one another is risen and walks among us. All that he taught — compassion, love, forgiveness, reconciliation, sincerity, selflessness for the sake of others — is vindicated and affirmed if he is truly risen. While the Easter mystery does not deny the reality of suffering and pain, it does proclaim reason for hope in the human condition. The empty tomb of Christ trumpets the ultimate *Alleluia* — that love, compassion, generosity, humility and selflessness will ultimately triumph over hatred, bigotry, prejudice, despair, greed and death. The Easter miracle enables us, even in the most difficult and desperate of times, to live our lives in hopeful certainty of the fulfillment of the resurrection at the end of our life's journey.

Throughout the forty days of Lent we have been steering our lives toward the light, trying to shake the darkness, the doubts, the burdens of living, the heaviness of hearts. May Easter become a verb in our lives — a way of living, a way of loving, a way of seeing and hearing and understanding. Let us not just celebrate this Easter day, but let us "do" Easter every day. Let us not just mark this milestone of the life of the Gospel Jesus, but let this day mark our lives with the compassion, humility and joy of the Risen One. Let us "easter" every moment of our lives in the light of Christ.

"Easter" in us, O Risen Christ,
that your Resurrection may become a way of living,
a way of loving,
a way of seeing and hearing and understanding.
In your light, may we "easter"
in every moment and day and season:
living in the hope of your constant presence
        in our midst,
lifting up one another in your forgiveness and grace,
building your kingdom of justice and peace
        in this world
as we struggle on our way to the world to come.
Let us not just celebrate this Easter day,
but let us "do" Easter every day.
May this Easter illuminate our lives
with the light of your compassion, justice and peace.

Second Sunday of Easter

"Peace be with you. As the Father has sent me, so I send you. And when he said this he breathed upon them and said to them, "Receive the Holy Spirit ... "
Jesus said to Thomas, "Put your finger here and see my hands, and bring your hand and put it into my side, and do not be unbelieving, but believe."

John 20: 19–31

Reunion

You met each other your first day on campus. Some of you were assigned to be roommates; some of you exchanged quick hellos on that awkward September afternoon as you moved into the dorm or you connected during the various orientation sessions. You got to know each other through classes, sharing tables in the cafeteria, during breaks while studying at night in the library.

Thrown into the excitement and terror of the college experience, your friendship helped you all survive. Together, you forged your way through the next four years: unfathomable lectures, mysterious lab experiments, autocratic professors, midnight cramming sessions. You held one another up through broken romances and on the mornings after the nights before. You toasted one another's grad school acceptances, first jobs and engagements.

Commencement did not end your friendship but deepened it. Over the years, you have always been there for one another, through good times and bad. You have celebrated one another's marriages, welcomed each other's children, mourned break-ups and helped one another cope with your first real experiences of death and loss. Each one of you knows that help, support and understanding are only a phone call away — always honest and blunt but never judgmental or condemning.

You are now older, grayer and wiser than that first week of classes. Those who are able gather for your official college reunions; sometimes you will meet for dinner when passing through somebody's town.

A new cycle of gatherings began not too long ago: coming together for the funerals of your parents. The next cycle will begin soon: gathering for the weddings of your children. Throughout the year there are telephone calls, Christmas letters — the ones you actually look forward to reading — and e-mail. Whenever any of you get together, your friendship picks up exactly where you last left off, as if you had just gotten together after class.

These friendships are centered on trust, acceptance, understanding and generosity. But the single most important element binding you together as friends is your shared memory of those four critical years in your young lives: you remember with one another and for one another the struggles of adulthood, the lessons of loves lost, the importance of not taking ourselves too seriously. Those memories now help you navigate through marriage, parenthood and middle age and beyond.

Shared memories are what bind individuals together as family, friends and community. In our memories of the events at which our lives intersect, we define our identity, we discover the meaning and purpose of our lives, we find a helping hand and a listening ear as we make our way through the next chapters of our loves.

It is a shared memory that binds us together as a church, as well. We trace our roots as a parish community to that Easter night when the Risen Jesus appears to the terrified disciples and "breathes" his Spirit of peace upon them. From that moment on, they — and we — are bound together by the living memory of Jesus as the new Israel, the Church of the Risen One.

The two stories that make up today's Gospel mirror the Church the Risen Jesus envisions.

The first story takes place on Easter night. The terrified disciples are huddled together behind locked doors. They are marked men because of their association with the criminal Jesus. The Risen Jesus appears in their midst with his greeting of "Peace." John clearly has the Genesis story in mind when the evangelist describes Jesus as "breathing" the Holy Spirit on his disciples: Just as God created man and woman by breathing life into them (Genesis 2: 7), the Risen Christ re-creates humankind by breathing the new life of the Holy Spirit upon the eleven.

The "peace" that Christ gives his new Church is not a sedative of good feeling or the simple absence of conflict or hostility. Christ's peace is active and transforming; it re-creates and renews. It is peace that is born of gratitude and humility, peace that values the hopes and dreams and needs of another over one's own, peace that welcomes back the lost, heals the brokenhearted, and respects the dignity of every man, woman and child as a son and daughter of God. Christ's peace is hard work; creating and maintaining the peace of Christ requires focused and determined action.

Jesus' "breathing" his spirit of peace and reconciliation upon his frightened disciples transformed them into a new creation, the Church. Jesus' gift of peace and his entrusting to his disciples the work of forgiveness defines the very identity of a church, a parish, a community of faith: to accept one another, to affirm one another, to support one another as God has done for us in the Risen Christ. What brought the Eleven and the first Christians together as a community — unity of heart, missionary witness, prayer, works of charity, a commitment to reconciliation and forgiveness — no less powerfully binds us to one another as the Church of the Risen Christ today.

Which brings us to the story of Thomas. The disciples excitedly tell the just-returned Thomas of what they had seen. Thomas responds to the news with understandable skepticism. A week later, Jesus returns to the gathering of disciples — this time with Thomas present. He invites Thomas to examine his wounds and to "believe." Christ's blessing in response to Thomas' profession of faith exalts the faith of every Christian of every age who "believes without seeing," who realizes and celebrates the presence of the Risen Christ in their midst by living lives of Gospel compassion, justice and forgiveness.

All of us, at one time or another, experience the doubt and skepticism of Thomas: While we have heard the good news of Jesus' empty tomb, all of our fears, problems and sorrows prevent us from realizing it in our own lives. But the signs of resurrection are all around us: the "nail marks" of sufferings endured that have led to the victory of justice and righteousness; empty tombs from which souls dead to fear and hopelessness have risen to new possibilities. Our own passion experiences calls us to move beyond the betrayals and injustices that we have endured. With an openness of heart and generosity of spirit, with persevering faith in God's ever-present grace, wonderful things are possible, dreams worthy of our hope can be realized, resurrection can take place in our own time and place. As Thomas experiences, Easter transforms our crippling sense of skepticism and cynicism into a sense of trust and hope in providence of God. The power of the Resurrection transcends time and place.

Our identity as the Church is centered in the memory of Jesus, God's Christ. Together, in word and sacrament, we celebrate the living presence of Jesus, the Lamb of God who re-creates us in the love of God in his passion, death and resurrection. Together, in our work for reconciliation and justice, we realize the peace of God in our midst. Together, in lifting one another up and supporting each other on our journey to eternity, we heal and are healed by God's living Word of forgiveness and healing.

*R*isen Jesus,
may we always find joy and hope,
    purpose and direction,
in our living the memory of your life in our midst.
May the "breath" of your Spirit of peace
transform us into your church of peace,
    ministers of your forgiveness
    and witnesses of your resurrection
    to our broken, crucified world.

> Jesus opened their minds to understand the Scriptures: "Thus it is written that the Christ would suffer and rise from the dead on the third day and that repentance, for the forgiveness of sins, would be preached in his name to all the nations, beginning from Jerusalem. You are witnesses of these things."

Luke 24: 35–48

The next great idea

*I*magine you have discovered the cure for a horrible disease.

Or you have come up with a workable design for an automobile that operates solely on sunlight.

Or you have devised that next generation of computers.

You would be unstoppable in bringing your concept to reality. Convinced of the workability and feasibility of your compound or conveyance or device, everything you have — time, energy, money — would go into perfecting your idea and convincing the medical community, Detroit, investment bankers to buy into your idea.

But you would be much more than a seller or a marketer. You would be articulating a vision, you would be igniting a revolution. For you have not just heard about the future, you have seen it, you have touched it, you have created it.

To be a witness of Christ is not simply to repeat what we have heard but to give our whole lives as evidence of that truth. Belief in the resurrected Lord can't be argued or explained in words. Even Jesus didn't try that. He knew that the truth of his resurrection had to be seen, had to be touched, had to be experienced in the flesh. We are witnesses when we can invite someone to look into our homes, our families, our friendships, our work, our checkbooks, our day-timers — and find Jesus there.

Today's Gospel is the conclusion of Luke's account of Jesus' first post-resurrection appearance to his disciples. The two disciples who met Jesus on the road to Emmaus have returned to Jerusalem to confirm the women's story of the resurrection. While they are excitingly telling their story, Jesus appears.

Luke goes to great lengths in his Easter accounts to make clear that the resurrection was neither the fantasy of crazy zealots nor a plot concocted by the disciples who somehow managed to spirit the body of Jesus away (according to Luke's account, the disciples themselves had not gone near the tomb themselves or even expected any kind of "resurrection"). In the details he presents here, Luke is countering the arguments forwarded to explain away the resurrection myth. There can be no mistake: The resurrection of Jesus Christ is a reality, a reality in which all of the Scriptures find their ultimate fulfillment.

For Luke, the power of Jesus' resurrection is realized in the way it "opens" one's heart and mind to understanding the deeper meaning of God's Word and to fully embracing the Spirit of God. In our faith and trust in the Risen Christ, we become "witnesses" of the mercy and forgiveness of God.

In the passion, death and resurrection of Jesus, God reveals in a specific moment of history, in a specific location on earth, his limitless and eternal love for his people. The Easter miracle is God's assurance that love and forgiveness, even in the most difficult situations, are never offered in vain; in finding the ability to cope without losing hope, in learning from the painful realities of life and in accepting the lessons learned in God's Spirit of humility and patience, we become capable of growth, re-creation, transformation — and resurrection. God continues to make the miracle of the empty tomb present to us in the caring, compassion and love we receive and give — the love we have witnessed in the suffering of Christ, a love that is victorious even over death.

*I*n the spring light of this Easter season, O Lord,
may we recognize your presence in our midst
in the flesh and bone of one another.
May we see you in the eyes of one another;
may we hear your voice in the cries of one another,

may we see your scars in the hurts we can heal.
May the fish we share with the hungry
and our bread that we break with the poor
be our witness to hope in your promise
   of the Resurrection
for all your beloved sons and daughters,
our sisters and brothers in you.

Fourth Sunday of Easter

"A hired man, who is not a shepherd and whose sheep are not his own, sees a wolf coming and leaves the sheep and runs away, and the wolf catches and scatters them ... "I am the good shepherd, and I know mine and mine know me ... I will lay down my life for the sheep."

John 10:11–18

Negotiating the rocky terrain

A rabbi who has prepared many couples for marriage shares the wisdom of his years of experience:

"Think of two married couples. One couple insists that they have never had a serious quarrel in all the years they have been married. They have never spoken a harsh word to each other. Each considers the other his or his best friend in the world. The other couple has lost count of the number of angry, screaming, ashtray-throwing fights they have had. Time and again, they have found themselves wondering if their relationship had a future. But every time they pondered the option of separation, they would peer into the abyss and step back from it. They would remember how much they had shared and realize how much they cared for each other. Which relationship would you think to be stronger, more able to survive an unanticipated downturn or sudden tragedy? I would have more confidence in the second couple, who have been taught by experience how strong the bond between them is."[1]

In the work of "shepherding," sometimes we are the shepherd who reaches out to the one lost or in trouble and, at other times, we are the one in distress in need of a shepherd's saving grab. In Christ, we belong to one another; in imitating Christ, our lives are at the service of one another. "Good shepherding" is not dominating or patronizing nor is it for the weak and self-absorbed; "good shepherding" is selfless and generous work that realizes with gratitude that we are sometimes the shepherd and sometimes the struggling and lost.

Jesus' figure of the Good Shepherd is not an idyllic, serene image. Palestinian shepherds were held absolutely liable for every single sheep entrusted to their care; "good" shepherds, motivated by a sense of responsibility rather than money, considered it a matter of honor to lay down their lives for the sheep in their charge, taking on every kind of wild beast and marauder in defense of the flock.

While the shepherd/sheep metaphor is well known throughout Scripture, Jesus' vow to lay down his life for his sheep is something new. It completes Jesus' break with the mercenary religious leaders of the establishment who care little for the flock they have been entrusted to serve.

Jesus the Good Shepherd calls us to look beyond our own expectations, needs and fears in order to become "shepherds" of reconciliation, compassion and charity to others. To be a disciple of Jesus is not to be simply a "hired hand" who acts only to be rewarded; real followers of Jesus realize that every person of the "one fold" possesses the sacred dignity of being children of God and rejoice in knowing that in serving others we serve God. In embracing the Gospel attitude of humility and compassion for the sake of others — in "laying down our own lives" for others — our lives will one day be "taken up again" in the Father's Easter promise.

*J*esus the Good Shepherd,
guide our steps over the crags and rocky terrain
    of our lives,
and bring us safely to the pasture
of your wisdom and grace.
Make us selfless shepherds to one another,
that we may walk with them through the gate
of your peace and compassion.

Fifth Sunday of Easter

"I am the true vine, and my Father is the vine grower ... I am the vine, you are the branches ... Whoever does not abide in me is thrown away like a branch and withers; such branches are gathered, thrown into the fire, and burned."

'Why I Make Sam Go To Church'

Sam is the only kid he knows who goes to church. But Mom insists.

Mom is writer Anne Lamott, who has chronicled her own search for God in her troubled life in her bestselling books, including *Grace Eventually* and *Plan B*. In *Traveling Mercies: Some Thoughts on Faith*, Mom explains why she wants her poor little Presbyterian church to be part of her son's life:

"I want to give him what I found in the world, a path and a little light to see by. Most of the people I know who have what I want — which is to say, purpose, heart, balance, gratitude, joy — are people with a deep sense of spirituality. They are people in community, who pray, or practice their faith ... They follow a brighter light than the glimmer of their own candle.

"When I was at the end of my rope, the people of St. Andrew tied a knot in it for me and helped me to hold on. The church became my home — that's where, when you show up, they have to let you in. They let me in. They even said, You come back now.

"Sam was welcomed and prayed for at St. Andrew's seven months before he was born. When I announced during worship that I was pregnant, people cheered. All these old people, raised in Bible-thumping homes in the Deep South, clapped. Even the women whose grown-up boys had been or were doing time in jails or prisons rejoiced for me ... Women [who] live pretty close to the bone financially on small Social Security checks ... routinely sidled up to me and stuffed bills in my pockets — tens and twenties ... And then almost immediately they set about providing for us. They brought clothes, they brought me casseroles to keep in the freezer, they brought me assurance that this baby was going to be part of the family.

"I was usually filled with a sense of something like shame until I'd remember that wonderful line of Blake's — that we are here to learn to endure the beams of love — and I would take a long breath and force these words out of my strangled throat: Thank you."[2]

Today's Gospel calls us to realize the connections between Christ and us and between us and one another. On the night before he died (the setting of today's Gospel) Jesus reminds his disciples of every time and place that, in his love, we are "grafted" to one another in ways we do not completely realize or understand. From the music of the psalms to the engravings on the temple pediments, vines were a symbol of Yahweh's many blessings to Israel. Jesus appropriates the image of the vine to explain his eternal connectedness to his disciples, their connectedness through him to God, and their connectedness to one another.

As branches of Christ the vine, we are part of something greater than ourselves, something which transforms and transcends the fragileness of our lives. In Christ, we are "grafted" to God and to one another. In Christ, the son of a single, white mother "belongs" to the elderly black widow in the next bench; in Christ, the small country church is one with the great city cathedral. The Risen One calls us all to community, to be branches on the same vine, to realize our life in Christ is also life in one another.

*B*ring us together, Risen Christ,
   into the life of your vine.
Grafted to one another in the love of God breathed
   into us,
connected to one another in the waters of Baptism,
may we bring to fruition the yield of this vine:
the wine of peace,
the fruit of compassion,
the harvest of justice.

Sixth Sunday of Easter

"This is my commandment: Love one another as I have loved you."

Loving Robbie

*T*here are some people who are easy to love. You want to help them. You're uplifted by their genuine gratitude.

And then there are people like Robbie. Robbie wore out her welcome with the social service agencies a long time ago. Robbie's poverty is real, her life is hard — but she runs through help like water.

The Rev. Lawrence Wood was the pastor of Robbie's local church. Writing in *The Christian Century*, the Reverend Wood remembers one winter Friday when Robbie called the church repeatedly to ask for groceries. The pastor invited her to come to the food kitchen. She didn't have a car — couldn't someone drive some food out her way? "I haven't had anything to eat for four days," she moaned. Folks who come to the pantry usually take whatever the church has in stock, but Robbie had a shopping list: smoked turkey, lean roast beef and a pound of coffee — decaf.

A bad storm had dumped a foot of snow on the community. The pastor didn't want to saddle someone else with Robbie so late on a Friday, so he went to the food pantry, filled a few grocery sacks and drove the 20 miles out to her place, muttering under his breath the whole time.

Robbie's place was a shambles. No one had shoveled or plowed. Seeing the pastor coming, Robbie stepped out of her door smoking a cigarette. "Did you bring the coffee?" she called out. "Decaf?"

The minister stopped about 20 yards from her door. The snow was deep.

"Could you pull up a little closer?"

"Robbie, just stay there," the Reverend Wood shouted back and waded through the drifts with one sack, then the other, then the next, feeling the burden on his lower back.

Robbie beamed, but before a conversation could begin, the pastor said, "Well, that's about it," and left without asking anything about her or what she might need. It was not one of his better days in ministry.

But Pastor Wood remembers that on the trip home "I did feel lighter. In spite of myself, I felt glad to be of help. And about a hundred yards down the road, I had the odd feeling that when I am judged, it will be by what I do for Robbie."[3]

Love one another — it's not a suggestion but a command. *Love one another* — there are no qualifications, conditions or limitations. *Love another* — even the mean-spirited, the petulant, the ungrateful, the unreasonable. Christ calls us to love as he has loved us: to bring healing and peace into every life we touch.

Continuing last Sunday's theme of the vine and branches (from his Last Supper discourse in John's Gospel), Jesus speaks of the love of God as the bonding agent of the new Israel. The model of love for the faithful disciple — "to love one another as I have loved you" — is extreme, limitless and unconditional. The love manifested in the Gospel and the resurrection of Christ creates an entirely new relationship between God and humanity. Again Christ, the obedient Servant Redeemer, is the great "connector" between God and us.

This is the commandment that Jesus entrusts to us who would be his Church: to love one another as Jesus, God made human, has loved us. As Christ gave himself for others, we are to imitate his example of service to others; as Christ brought healing and peace into the lives of those he encountered, we are to bring that same healing and peace into the lives we touch; as Christ revealed to the world a God who loves humanity as a parent loves his children, we are to love one another as brothers and sisters.

Christ also transforms creation's relationship with its Creator. God is not the distant, aloof, removed architect of the universe;

God is not the cruel taskmaster; God is not the unfeeling judge who seeks the destruction of the wicked. God is creative, reconciling, energizing love — and Jesus is the perfect expression of that love.

All that God has done in the first creation of Genesis and the re-creation of Easter has been done out of limitless, unfathomable, sacred love. Such love invites us to a relationship with God centered in friendship, not fear; such love calls us to put aside our self-loathing over our unworthiness and failings and embrace, instead, a spirit of grateful joy for what God has done for us and in us.

May we see in the Robbies, who wear us down in their demanding neediness, the face of Christ and know that in loving the Robbies around us we express the love of Christ who lived for us, died for us, and rose for us.

*L*ord Jesus, you have called us your "friends"
and have entrusted to us your work
   of compassion and peace.
Inspired by your example of selflessness and
animated by your spirit of humility,
may we love one another,
especially when such love is most difficult,
undeserved, and unappreciated,
remembering that you continue to love us —
despite ourselves.

The Ascension of the Lord

The Lord Jesus was taken up into heaven and took his seat at the right hand of God. But they went forth and preached everywhere while the Lord worked with them and confirmed the word through accompanying signs.

Mark 16: 15–20

" … you will receive power when the Holy Spirit comes upon you, and you will be my witnesses in Jerusalem, throughout Judea and Samaria, and to the ends of the earth."

Acts 1: 1–11

'Griots' of the Lord

*I*n his landmark book *Roots,* Alex Haley tells the story of his ancestors, beginning with Kunte Kinte, who was kidnapped from his African homeland and brought to America as a slave in the 18th century.

Haley first heard the stories about "Kin-tay" from his grandmother. To research the book he traveled to Africa to talk with the *griots* — the storytellers who kept alive the centuries-old oral history of their villages and tribes. Haley eventually found the old griot in his ancestral village who could confirm his grandmother's tales about Kunte Kinte. Haley wrote:

"The old man sat me down, facing me … Then he began to recite for me the ancestral history of the Kinte clan … I was struck not only by the profusion of details, but also by the narrative's Biblical style, something like 'so-and-so took as his wife so-and-so, and they begat … '"

Two hours after he began, the griot came to the name Haley had traveled thousands of miles to hear: "Omorrow Kinte begat Kunte … Kunte went away from his village to chop wood...and he was never seen again."

The author remembered:

"I sat as if I were carved of stone. My blood seemed to have congealed. This man whose lifetime has been spent in this back-country African village had no way in the world to know that he had just echoed what I had heard all through my boyhood years on my grandma's porch in Kenning, Tennessee ... of an African who always insisted that his name was 'Kin-tay'; who had called a guitar a 'ko,' and a river within the state of Virginia, 'Kamby Bolongo'; and who had been kidnapped into slavery while not far from his village, chopping wood, to make himself a drum."[4]

Christ calls us, in his Ascension Day commission, to be his *griots* — to teach his Word to our children and to our children's children, to tell his story to our families and friends through our commitment to what is right, our sense of compassion and caring in our dealings with others, our ethical and moral approach to business in the marketplace, our sense of awareness and gratitude for all that God has done for us.

Today's readings include two accounts of Jesus' return to the Father:

Reading 1 is the beginning of the Acts of the Apostles, Luke's "Gospel of the Holy Spirit." Jesus' Ascension begins volume two of Luke's work. The words and images here evoke the First Covenant accounts of the ascension of Elijah (2 Kings 2) and the forty years of the Exodus: Luke considers the time that the Risen Lord spent with his disciples a sacred time, a "desert experience" for the apostles to prepare them for their new ministry of preaching the Gospel of the resurrection. (Acts alone places the Ascension forty days after Easter; the synoptic Gospels — including, strangely, Luke's — specifically place the Ascension on the day of Easter; John writes of the "Ascension" not as an event but as a new existence with the Father.) Responding to their question about the restoration of Israel, Jesus discourages his disciples from guessing what cannot be known. Greater things await them as his "witnesses." In the missionary work before them, Christ will be with them in the presence of the Spirit to come.

Scholars call today's Gospel the "longer ending" of Mark's text. In style and substance, these six verses are very unlike Mark;

the best guess is that these verses were added sometime in the first century to "complete" Mark's account to include the tradition of the Ascension of Jesus. Before returning to the Father, Jesus commissions his new church to continue Christ's presence on earth through their proclamation of the "good news."

Christ places his Church in the care of a rag-tag collection of fishermen, tax collectors and peasants — and yet, what began with those Eleven has grown and flourished through the centuries to our own parish family and faith community. The Church Jesus leaves to them is rooted not in buildings or wealth or formulas of prayer or systems of theology but in faith nurtured in the human heart, a faith centered in joy and understanding that is empowering and liberating, a faith that gives us the strength and freedom to be authentic and effective witnesses of the Risen One, who is present among us always.

The words Jesus addresses to his disciples on the mountain of the Ascension are addressed to all of us two millennia later. We are called to teach, to witness and to heal in our own small corners of the world, to hand on to others the story that has been handed on to us about Jesus and his Gospel of love and compassion.

May we always realize your presence in our midst,
O Risen Lord,
as we struggle to go forth
and do the work you have entrusted to us:
to teach others, in the example of our lives,
your Gospel of justice and forgiveness,
to reveal to our world
your compassion in our midst,
to be architects of your peace,
    bringing all nations and peoples together
    under your commandment of love.

[In some churches and dioceses, the Ascension of the Lord is celebrated on the Seventh Sunday of Easter.]

Seventh Sunday of Easter

"Holy Father, keep them in your name that you have given me, so that they may be one, just as we are one ... Consecrate them in the truth; your word is truth. As you sent me into the world, so I sent them into the world."

John 17: 11–19

Connect the dots

You are standing on the summit of a beautiful mountain or a great rocky crag overlooking the majestic ocean; or you have the opportunity to witness the awesome color of a sunset in the Southwest desert; or you are spending a quiet spring morning fishing for trout in a crystal clear stream. You can't help but sense the greatness of God in such natural beauty and wonder how anyone could let thoughtless pollution or ill-planned development destroy such sacredness. And as you make your way home you leave behind your empty soda cans, candy wrappers and cigarette butts.

Connect the dots.

We are all concerned about health issues. We don't feel as well as we should; we're always tired; stress hangs over us like a shroud. Yet we smoke too much, exercise too little, drink with abandon and eat with little thought to exactly *what* we are eating.

Connect the dots.

We work too hard, we have no time for the really important things of life. But we never say no to another meeting, to a new project, to the opportunity for more overtime. We want time for family and friends, for prayer and quiet, but, truth be told, a blank or barely-filled page in our calendar book terrifies us.

Connect the dots.

We all want only the best for our children. We want to protect them from the "bad" things out there; we want them to be able to make their way through life as happy, good and loving men and women. But the time necessary to become a family is lost in a sea of work, school and sports schedules; everything — from our relationships with one another to our relationship with God — is on the run.

Connect the dots.

So why are things such a mess? Why do we feel so detached from the people who mean most to us? Why do we feel so empty, so unfulfilled?

Come on — *connect the dots.*

The call to discipleship demands the courage and integrity to *connect the dots* — to embrace the truth and pay the price of living it and proclaiming it. Only when we start to connect the dots can we begin to transform our lives, our communities, our world.

We are often too willing to bend, shape, rework, edit, manipulate and rationalize the facts to fit our own concept of "truth"; true discipleship, however, calls us to seek out and embrace the Gospel's unvarnished proclamation of truth centered in the unconditional love of God and the sacredness of every human being as created in the image and life of God.

In John's account of the Last Supper, after his final teachings to his disciples before his passion, Jesus addresses his Father in heaven. Today's Gospel is from Chapter 17 of John's Gospel, the "high priestly prayer" of Jesus in which he prays for his disciples, that they may be united in love, persevere despite the world's "hatred" of them for the Word that they will proclaim, and be "consecrated" in the "truth." Jesus asks for his disciples of every place and time the courage and integrity to embrace the "light" of truth — to recognize the hand of God in all things, to embrace the life of God "breathing" in every human interaction, to realize the sacredness of every human being as created in the image and life of God.

The Gospel challenges us to recognize the prejudices, biases and ambitions that exist within each one of us and to realize how they affect our perception of the "truth" and the decisions we make based on that perception. We are called to uphold, regardless of the cost, the holiness of "truth" — truth that is rooted in the reality of God's love and in the sacredness of every person as created in the image and life of God.

*G*racious God,
open our eyes to recognize you and your truth
    in all things.
Open our hearts to accept what is good
    and right and just despite the costs.
Open our spirits to know the freedom and joy
    that is ours
    in embracing your Spirit of mercy and compassion.
Open our mouths to give voice to that truth,
that justice,
that mercy,
that compassion in our midst.

Pentecost

The disciples were filled with the Holy Spirit and began to speak in other languages as the Spirit gave them ability.

Acts 2: 1–11

Jesus breathed on them and said, "Receive the Holy Spirit."

John 20: 19–23

'Yes, I guess I can ... '

A platoon is on night patrol. Suddenly, shots ring out from the darkness. Everyone dives for cover. When the lieutenant gives the all-clear, everyone is OK — except one. The sniper has seriously wounded a member of the platoon. Instinctively, his buddies work together to stop the bleeding. Then they pair up, taking turns carrying him to an aid station — some ten miles away. If any one of them had ever thought about such a terrifying situation, they would never imagine they could save their buddy. But, somehow, they do. Love for a brother beats being scared to death every time.

It's spring break. Like thousands of college students, he's on a plane — but he's not heading to any place warm and fun. He's on his way to a rural town somewhere in the Appalachians. A group from his college signed up to help with a Habitat for Humanity project during the break. It seemed like a good idea at the time — but now he's not so sure. *I've never done anything like this before. I don't know how to build anything. What if I mess this up? What if the week is a total bust?* But the week will be anything but a bust — it turns out to be one of the most educational, enjoyable and fulfilling experiences of his life. *Yeh, I guess I can build something,* he discovers.

Marriage is a roller coaster of joys and sorrows, of triumphs and tragedies. Job losses, illnesses, and the myriad of challenges of raising a child are all part of the adventure. Just about every spouse faces some kind of complication that confronts them with their own inadequacies and doubts: *I can't do this. I can't be the husband or wife or father or mother I need to be.* And yet, they manage to find within themselves the love, the compassion, the forgiveness to be the spouse and parent their family needs them to be in that moment.

In each of the accounts of Pentecost, the Holy Spirit enables the disciples to do things they could not do on their own: In Acts, the Spirit empowers Peter and his brothers to speak boldly of the Risen Christ; in John's Gospel, Jesus "breathes" his Spirit upon the remnant in the upper room to help them understand and embrace the "truth" of his love — truth they could never bear or understand on their own.

That is Pentecost: the Spirit of God filling us, the Church of the Risen Christ, with the grace to do the work of compassion and forgiveness we can't imagine ourselves doing, the understanding to take on the work of his justice and peace despite our own fears and doubts.

Pentecost was the Jewish festival of the harvest (also called the Feast of Weeks), celebrated 50 days after Passover, when the first fruits of the corn harvest were offered to the Lord. A feast of pilgrimage (hence the presence in Jerusalem of so many "devout Jews of every nation"), Pentecost also commemorated Moses' receiving the Law on Mount Sinai. For the new Israel, Pentecost becomes the celebration of the Spirit of God's compassion, peace and forgiveness — the Spirit that transcends the Law and becomes the point of departure for the young Church's universal mission (the planting of a new harvest?).

In his Acts of the Apostles (Reading 1), Luke invokes the First Testament images of wind and fire in his account of the new Church's Pentecost: God frequently revealed his presence in fire (the pillar of fire in the Sinai) and in wind (the wind that sweeps over the earth to make the waters of the Great Flood subside). The Hebrew word for spirit, *ruah*, and the Greek word *pneuma* also refer to the movement of air, not only as wind, but also of life-giving breath (as in God's creation of man in Genesis 2 and the re-vivification of the dry bones in Ezekiel 37). Through his life-giving "breath," the Lord begins the era of the new Israel on Pentecost.

Today's Gospel, the first appearance of the Risen Jesus before his ten disciples (remember Thomas is not present) on Easter night, is John's version of the Pentecost event. In "breathing" the Holy Spirit upon them, Jesus imitates God's act of creation in Genesis. Just as Adam's life came from God, so the disciples' new life of the Spirit comes from Jesus. In the Resurrection, the Spirit replaces their sense of self-centered fear and confusion with the "peace" of understanding, enthusiasm and joy and shatters all barriers among them to make of them a community of hope and forgiveness. By Christ's sending them forth, the disciples become *apostles* — "those sent."

The feast of Pentecost celebrates the unseen, immeasurable presence of God in our lives and in our Church — the *ruah* of God that animates us to do the work of the Gospel of the Risen One, the *ruah* that makes God's will our will, the *ruah* of God living in us and transforming us so that we might bring his life and love to our broken world. God "breathes" his Spirit into our souls that we may live in his life and love; God ignites the "fire" of his Spirit within our hearts and minds that we may seek God in all things in order to realize the coming of his reign

May this Pentecost empower us with the grace of God to take on what we know is right and good and just — despite our own sense of inadequacy and failure; may we live in the conviction that the Spirit will enable us to do what is of and by God if we are willing to love enough to try.

*C*ome, Spirit of God.
and breathe your *ruah* into us.
that we might become the holy people
 you created us to be;
that we might love as you have loved us;
that we might create your reign of justice and peace
 in our own time and place;
that we might heal and comfort,
 forgive and restore,
 as did the Gospel Jesus.
May your "breath" enliven us
to do the work of the Gospel
and live the faith we have received.

Solemnities of the Lord in Ordinary Time

The Holy Trinity

"Go and make disciples of all nations, baptizing them in the name of the Father, and of the Son, and of the Holy Spirit, teaching them to observe all that I have commanded you."

Matthew 28: 16–20

The medicine pouch

A South African legend recounts the tale of a good king who ruled with great justice and wisdom. But a village in his kingdom was led by an arrogant, foolish chief who broke away from the king.

The king could have very easily destroyed the chief and his henchmen. But instead he sent a trusted messenger to the village. The emissary journeyed alone to meet with the rebel chief to express the king's concern for the breakaway village. Had the king oppressed them? Had he treated them badly or offended them in some way? What was wrong? How could this be made right?

The chief and the elders knew that they had no grievance against the good king; they tried to mask their embarrassment with anger. Despite their harsh words, the messenger remained calm — which infuriated the chief and elders even more. They became so infuriated and unnerved by the messenger's demeanor that they killed the messenger. Then, in a repulsive and despicable act, they sent to the king a clay pot filled with the murdered envoy's blood.

As news of the murder of the king's beloved advisor spread, everyone expected the king to send his warriors to destroy the evil village.

But that is not what the good king did.

The king took the blood and poured it on the great flat rock that served as the meeting place for the king and his people. In the hot African sun, the liquid blood soon dried into a powder.

The king then collected the powder into a medicine pouch made of lambskin. He sent the pouch to the rebellious village with this message:

"The blood of the messenger you killed is in this medicine pouch. It may bring you life or death. Though you killed him, I still invite you to come back into my kingdom on one condition. You must take some of the dry blood, mix it with water, and rub it on your hands. Then come and stand before me at the great flat rock and hold up your hands. In this way you will acknowledge your guilt in my messenger's death but that you now wish to be received back into my kingdom. If you trust my word and wear the blood of my messenger, his blood will be the means of reconciliation between us. There will be no punishment.

"But if you refuse to be reconciled by my messenger's blood, I shall send my warriors on you like locusts.

"The king has spoken. The medicine pouch is in your hands."[1]

This South African folktale mirrors the God of the Trinity whom we have encountered in both Scripture and in the human experience: God who is "Father" of all and "king" who unites all of humanity under his providence; God who is "Son" and "messenger" who reveals the compassion of God for us and, by his blood, reconciles us to God; and God who is "Spirit," the "medicine" of reconciliation and mercy offered to all by God.

Today we celebrate the essence of our faith as manifested in our lives, we praise God as God has revealed himself to us: the loving providence of the Creator who continually invites us back to him; the selfless servanthood of the Redeemer who "emptied" himself to become like us in order that we might become like him; the joyful love of the Spirit that is the unique unity of the Father and Son.

(Ordinary Time in the liturgical year resumes with the Solemnity of the Holy Trinity. Today's celebration originated in France in the eighth century and was adopted by the universal Church in 1334.)

In the Gospel pericope assigned for today, the Risen Jesus, on the mount of the Ascension, commissions his fledgling church to teach and baptize in the name of the Holy One who reveals himself as Father, Son and Spirit. In the Trinity we find our identity as the people of God. The core of all of Jesus' teaching is the revelation of God as Father to humanity: Our God seeks a relationship with humankind based not on the all-powerful Creator demanding homage from the lowly slaves he created but as a loving Parent who welcomes his own children back home.

The Solemnity of the Holy Trinity confronts us with God's "medicine pouch" — the realization of the limitless love of God for us and the decision before us every day of our lives to seek and embrace God's love in all things.

May we behold your presence, O God,
in all its wonders and grace,
in every moment of our lives,
May everything we do give praise to you
as Father:
    the loving Creator and Sustainer of all life;
as Son:
    the Word and Light of God made human for us;
as Spirit:
    the love that binds Father to Son,
    and we to you and to one another.

The Body and Blood of the Lord

Jesus took bread, said the blessing, broke it and gave it to them and said, "Take it; this is my body."
Then he took the cup, gave thanks and gave it to them, and they all drank from it. He said to them, "This is my blood of the covenant, which will be shed for many."

Mark 14: 12–16, 22–26

Becoming what we have received

*I*t begins as a seed in the field. The earth nurtures it, the rain nourishes it. The farmer works to bring the grain to harvest; he collects it and separates it from the chaff. A baker then grinds it and kneads it; the dough is baked until what was once seed becomes bread.

In the vineyard, the grapes on the vine are cared for as if they were precious gems. Blessed by the sun and rain, the grapes are collected by the gentle hand of the vintner and then pressed and stored. In God's good time, at the perfect moment, the precious liquid becomes wine.

Bread and wine, gifts of the earth, the work of human hands.

Bread and wine, now placed on our altar.

Bread and wine, the body and blood of our God, lovingly given to us in the Eucharist.

But the bread and wine is more than the gifts of God to his people; they are parables of what it means to become God's people.

Like seed, we are transformed from grain to flour through the creative love of God. Farmers and vintners — in the persons of parents, spouses, teachers, pastors, friends — have nurtured us and formed us. We struggle to finally grow up; we stumble along the way. Like grain that is baked into bread, like grapes that ferment into wine, we change and become complete not in spite of what we suffer but because of what we suffer. We are re-created in the water of baptism; we are transformed in the fire of the Spirit.

And like the many grapes that are pressed together into the unity of the sweet liquid that fills the chalice, our prayers and sacrifices, our acts of generosity, our work of reconciliation and forgiveness, our sacrifices for one another in imitation of Christ (who is both the vine and winemaker), makes us "church" — the wine of the sacrament of unity.

What we see on this table is ourselves. We are bread; we are wine. We are called to be the sacrament we receive.[2]

Today we celebrate Christ's gift of the Eucharist, the source and summit of our life together as the Church. The Solemnity of the Body and Blood of the Lord originated in the Diocese of Liège in 1246 as the feast of Corpus Christi. In the reforms of Vatican II, the feast was joined with the feast of the Precious Blood (July 1) to become the Solemnity of the Body and Blood of the Lord.

Today's Gospel is Mark's account of the Last Supper. At the Passover meal marking the First Covenant, Jesus, the Lamb of the New Covenant, institutes the New Passover of the Eucharist. The sacrament of the bread and wine blessed, broken and given by Christ that night in the Cenacle continues to be celebrated on our own parish table. Our coming to the table of the Eucharist is more than just reliving the memory of Christ's great sacrifice for our redemption — in sharing his "body" in the bread of the Eucharist we re-enter the inexplicable love of God who gives us eternal life in his Son, the Risen Christ; in drinking his "blood" in the wine of the Eucharist we take his life into the very core of our beings.

In the Eucharist, bread and wine are transformed by the Spirit of God into the body and blood of Christ; the sacrament we receive should transform us into sacraments, as well — sacraments of God's love for one another, signs of God's presence to our families and communities. As the Eucharist makes us Christ's church of reconciliation, the Eucharist makes each one of us a minister of reconciliation; as the Eucharist animates the Church with the life of Christ, the Eucharist animates our lives in the love and compassion of God.

"If you have received worthily," St. Augustine preached, "you become what you have received." In sharing the body of Christ, we become the body of Christ. If we partake of the one bread and cup, then we must be willing to become Eucharist for others — to make the love of Christ real for all.

*I*n the sacrament of your body and blood,
Christ Jesus,
may we become what we receive:
let us become the bread of your justice
and the wine of your compassion
for all who hunger for your presence
    in the poverty of their lives.

ORDINARY TIME

NOTE: The Sundays in this section are numbered according to both the Roman lectionary's designation of Sundays of the Year and the Common lectionary's designation of Sundays after the Epiphany and Propers (Sundays after Pentecost).

Second Sunday of the Year

John was standing with two of his disciples, and as he watched Jesus walk by, he exclaimed, "Look, here is the Lamb of God!" The two disciples heard him say this, and they followed Jesus. One of the two was Andrew, who found his brother Simon and said to him, "We have found the Messiah."

John 1: 35–42
[Roman lectionary]

Learning to 'behold'

A boy and his father were walking in the woods when the boy was startled by a spider. Instinctively, the boy swatted the insect and was about to kill it. But his father stopped him in time.

"Look," his dad said. The boy stopped, bent down and watched the spider. He was soon captivated as the little spider continued to spin its silken web between the branches of a small tree. His dad explained that spiders are not to be feared, that spiders are good for the environment, protecting us and the plants we depend on for food by consuming disease-carrying insects.

The boy now saw the spider with entirely new eyes. He no longer saw an ugly insect but was awestruck by the spider's unseen work in creation; the boy's fear of the spider had been transformed into understanding and respect. The boy had come to realize the little spider's connection to his own life.

The youngster had learned to *behold* ...[1]

The word *behold* means more than just to "look" — to *behold* is to be caught up in wonder, attentiveness and awe, to realize and understood deeper than what merely "appears" on the surface. In today's Gospel (from John 1), John the Baptizer leaves the Gospel stage, exhorting his followers — and us — not just to "see" Jesus in our midst, but to "behold" his presence: to put aside our fears and stop our constant busyness in order to be transformed and re-created in the light of Christ. In John's proclamation of Jesus as the "Lamb of God," the age of the prophets ends and the era of the Messiah begins.

Jesus' invitation to Andrew to "Come and see" so moves Andrew that he invites his brother Simon Peter to "come and see" for himself. This is the first of three episodes in John's Gospel in which Andrew introduces someone to Christ: Andrew brings to Jesus the lad with the five barley loaves and a couple of dried fish (John 6: 8–9) and it is Andrew who asks Jesus to meet the Greeks who have requested, "Sir, we would like to meet Jesus" (John 12: 22).

In this new liturgical year, let us "behold" the Lamb of God among us: to open our hearts and consciences to see and hear Christ working, healing, and preaching in our midst; to embrace and be embraced by the love of God that moves and animates this story of his beloved Son's living among us.

*C*hrist Jesus,
open our eyes and unlock hearts
to behold your presence in our midst –
help us to look at the world with a vision of hope;
help us to recognize the dignity of every human being
    as your son and daughter;
help us to embrace and be embraced by your love
moving and living among us
    in our own Jerusalems and Nazareths.

Second Sunday of the Year /
Second Sunday after the Epiphany

Philip found Nathanael and told him, "We have found the one about whom Moses wrote in the law, and also the prophets, Jesus, son of Joseph, from Nazareth."
But Nathanael said to him, "Can anything good come from Nazareth?"
Philip said to him, "Come and see."

John 1: 43–51
[Common lectionary]

God in unexpected places

You can't help but hear the sneer in Nathanael's voice in today's Gospel. When Philip invites his friend to come and meet Jesus, Nathanael, reflecting the prevailing belief of the time that equated social status with one's place of birth, caustically replies, "Can anything good come from Nazareth?"

Come on, Phil! Nazareth? That backwater? It's a couple of farms in the middle of nowhere! There's nothing there, Phil, NOTHING!

If we learn anything from the Christmas gospels, it is that God can be found in the most unexpected of places. God is present in the poverty of our Bethlehems, in the emptiness of our Nazareths, in the turmoil of our Bethsaidas. God reveals himself in the generosity of a volunteer worker in a soup kitchen, in the patience of a teacher tutoring a struggling student, in the understanding of a high school senior who befriends the kid nobody else has time for. God's peace transforms our most challenging moments into occasions of grace; God's compassion illuminates our darkest nights with reason to hope and a sense of direction.

After the beautiful Prologue to his Gospel, the evangelist John recounts a series of brief scenes that serve as an introduction to his Gospel's "Book of Signs." In the course of four days, Jesus organizes his ministry in a series of encounters with John the Baptist (day one and two), Andrew and Simon (day three), and, in today's reading, Philip and Nathanael (day four). Each of these encounters provides a testimonial to the divinity of this Jesus: Lamb of God, Messiah, Son of God, King of Israel. The evangelist seeks to impress this Christology in the minds of his readers as he begins his narrative.

In today's pericope, Philip, who has been called by Jesus, approaches Nathanael. Nathanael provides a bit of vinegar to the story with his caustic remark, "Can anything good come out of Nazareth?" Nathanael's gibe (probably reflecting the rivalry typical between towns and regions) might also be included by John as a preview of the later rejection of Jesus by the Jewish establishment because of his origins.

Nathanael also serves as the model of the "true Israelite," part of the "remnant" who has faithfully awaited the fulfillment of God's reign in the coming of the Messiah and now sees that hope fulfilled in Jesus.

(Some scholars believe that Nathanael continued in Jesus' company as one of the Twelve. They suggest, though there is no conclusive evidence, that Nathanael is the apostle identified as "Bartholomew" in several New Testament lists of the apostles because Bartholomew's name follows that of Philip.)

Whatever Nathanael-like skepticism, biases and judgments we possess are shattered in the dawning of God's Christ. Often, to our surprise, God seeks us out from the isolation of our fig trees and invites us to come and realize a life transformed in his Christ.

May the light of your grace illuminate our hearts,
O God of compassion,
dispelling the darkness of skepticism and cynicism,
and opening our hearts to behold you
    in the most unexpected places.
Open our eyes and hearts to behold your presence
in every place, every moment and every heart.

Third Sunday of the Year /
Third Sunday after Epiphany

Jesus came to Galilee, proclaiming the good news about God, and saying, "The time is fulfilled, and the kingdom of God has come near; repent, and believe in the good news."
As Jesus passed along the Sea of Galilee, he saw Simon and his brother Andrew casting a net into the sea. "Follow me, and I will make you fishers of men."

Mark 1: 14–20

What's in a kiss ...

A mom learns about the power of a mother's kiss:

"My youngest daughter always had me kissing her boo-boos. I did it because, as every mother knows, it makes it feel better. What I never understood was the thought process behind the action.

"One day my daughter asked me to kiss her boo-boo when I was pressed for time, so I hurriedly obliged. She cried, telling me it wasn't any good because my kiss didn't have any love in it. I realized that kissing boo-boos was really about loving the pain away.

"This simple truth, along with the value of mindfulness my daughter taught me, has encouraged me to slow down, to become more aware and present in the moment. Slowing down is a conscious decision to live at a gentler pace and to make the most of the time I have.

"When my own mother passed away, I did not forget the love she gave me; it will live on in my heart forever. She gave me life, but beyond that, she gave me love ...

"With that errant kiss, I realized it was my responsibility as a mother to watch over my child's spiritual growth ... By simply showing my child kindness through listening, I believe I have satisfied my child's earliest spiritual needs. By being genuine

— that is, personally connected and physically present — I have satisfied my child's developing spirit."[2]

Parents mirror today's Gospel call to be "fishers" of others.

Jesus begins his ministry by calling simple fishermen to be his most trusted friends. Although the Twelve were hardly scholars or men wise in the ways of the world, Jesus sees beyond their gruff simplicity to call forth from them faith, sincerity and integrity. As Mark's Gospel unfolds each Sunday this year, the first disciples will misunderstand Jesus (if not miss the point entirely), desert him and even deny and betray him. But Jesus entrusts to them, for all of humankind, the proclamation of his Gospel. We, too, are called by Christ to be his "fishers," to help one another discover the love of God in our midst.

Christ entrusts to each one of us — whether we are a fisherman or a mom — the work of discipleship: to extend, in whatever our circumstances, the love of God for all; to proclaim, in our own homes and communities, the compassion, the forgiveness, the justice of the Gospel. To be the "fishers" that Christ calls us to become is to "cast the net" of God's love that we have experienced upon the waters of our time and place, to reach out and grasp the hand of those who struggle and stumble, to "love" away the hurt and pain and fear of those we love.

*B*e the star by which we navigate our small boats,
Lord Jesus,
as we seek out the lost and forgotten
and bring them safely home.
Guide our hands as we cast our small nets
    into the vast waters,
that we may realize a bounty of hope and grace
as we fish the rough seas of our lives.

Fourth Sunday of the Year /
Fourth Sunday after Epiphany

The people were astonished at Jesus' teaching, for he taught them as one having authority and not as the scribes: *"What is this? A new teaching with authority. He commands even the unclean spirits and they obey him."*

Mark 1: 21–28

The 'authority' of inspiration

*M*ost of us had one special teacher who challenged us to achieve more than we imagined ourselves capable of reaching, who inspired us to learn and discover not because of the grade we would receive but because of the knowledge and insight we would gain. They saw something in us that we did not realize we possessed; they called out of us new abilities and skills that would serve us for a lifetime. Such teachers and professors inspired their students by the wisdom of their examples, by genuine love of the teaching profession and their caring and their unconditional acceptance of their students.

Or, early in your career, you might have had a boss whose influence still has a powerful impact on your life — the kind of boss who treats those under him or her as coworkers instead of minions, who wins the respect of employees through the boss' clear respect for them; a boss who passed on a respect for the profession or trade; a boss who demanded competence, integrity and responsibility above all else — and taught you, too, to accept nothing less from yourself or from anybody else. From such a mentor you learned not only about your profession and business but about life, as well.

Or it might have been a coach or youth leader or sister or priest who had a profound influence on your life.

It might have been an aunt or uncle or older brother or sister. Or your mom and dad.

They showed you the right way to play the game … the right way to work a tool … the right way to finger the chord or sketch a line … the right way to treat another person. Through their compassion, their dedication, their wisdom — and the way they actually lived those values — they touched your lives in a way that will never be forgotten.

Today's Gospel portrays Jesus as a teacher who possesses an "authority" immediately perceived by his hearers, an authority that is centered in the example of his own compassion and empathy for those he has been called to serve. Mark writes in today's Gospel that the people marveled at Jesus' teaching "as one having authority and not as the scribes." Such an authority comes not from the power to enforce but from the ability to inspire.

The "authority" of Rabbi Jesus silences both demons and scribes in today's Gospel. For the poor Jews of Jesus' time, the scribes were the voices of authority, the final arbiters of the Law in which God had revealed himself. Their interpretation of the Law was considered absolute. "Demons" are encountered several times in Mark's Gospel. Anything that the people of Jesus' time could not understand or explain, such as disease, mental illness or bizarre or criminal behavior, was considered the physical manifestations of the evil one — "demons" or "unclean spirits."

Jesus' casting out the unclean spirit from the man possessed silences the voices of the demons that plague humanity. In his compassionate outreach to the poor and sick, Jesus "silences" the scribes by redefining their understanding of authority: whereas the "authority" of the scribes' words is based solely on their perceived status and learnedness, the authority of Jesus is born of compassion, peace and justice. The casting out of the demons and his curing of the sick who come to him are but manifestations of the power and grace of his words.

Note that the people of the Bible viewed miracles differently than we do. While we, in our high technology, scientific approach to the world, dismiss miracles as some kind of disruption or "overriding" of the laws of nature, the contemporaries of Jesus saw miracles as signs of God's immediate activity in his creation. While we ask, *How could this happen?*, they asked, *Who is responsible?* Their answer was always the same: the God of all creation. Those who witnessed Jesus' healings, then, saw them as God directly touching their lives.

The "unclean spirit" that Jesus casts out of the poor man in today's Gospel serves as a symbol of the voice of evil that sometimes speaks within us — the voice of revenge, self-centeredness, self-righteousness, greed, anger. We can be "possessed" by "demons" who discourage us and plague us with fear when we consider the unpopular position that we know is right and just; or the "demon" of rationalization that falsely justifies actions — or inactions — we know in our heart of hearts is contrary to the spirit of the Gospel. The compassionate Jesus of today's Gospel speaks to those "unclean spirits" as well, offering us the grace and courage to cast them out of our minds and hearts forever.

As Mark makes clear throughout his narrative, Jesus' teachings would remain abstract ideas were it not for his actions and the Spirit of God that compels those actions. Jesus acted compassionately; he forgave and healed; he released the sick and troubled from the "demons" that possessed them. In doing these things, he made the love and mercy of God a reality for a world that knew only violence, oppression and injustice.

*L*ord of compassion,
may we speak your word of mercy and justice
through the "authority" of our attempts –
however small or hidden,
however limited their success or scope –
to live your word in our own Capernaums.
Let our actions to console, to lift up, to heal,
to drive out the "demons" and "unclean spirits"
    of fear, greed and arrogance among us,
reveal your compassion and forgiveness in our midst.

Fifth Sunday of the Year /
Fifth Sunday after Epiphany

Rising very early before dawn, Jesus left and went off to a deserted place, where he prayed. Simon and those who were with him pursued him and on finding him said, "Everyone is looking for you." Jesus told them, "Let us go to the nearby villages that I may preach there also. For this purpose I have come ... "
Jesus cured many who were sick with various diseases, and he drove out many demons, not permitting them to speak because they knew him.

Mark 1: 29–39

The Gospel according to Hawkeye

*I*n his memoir *Never Have Your Dog Stuffed — And Other Things I've Learned,* actor Alan Alda recounts often hilarious but sometimes poignant stories of growing up with his popular burlesque-star father and his loving but mentally ill mother. He writes about his own struggles trying to make it as an actor and writer in New York and Hollywood and about marrying and raising a family of his own.

Alda will be identified forever as Hawkeye Pierce in the landmark television series *M*A*S*H.* He remembers the first day of walking on to the *M*A*S*H* set to begin filming the series and trying to transform himself into a character that was so different from himself.

"[The] question that had been nagging at me, even tormenting me, since I first began to act: How can I be so captured by my own imagination that I can truly connect to both the person I'm playing and to the person I'm playing with ... ?

"I didn't know it, but what I was really looking for was compassion. Not consciously, of course. I didn't consciously want to become compassionate. Who in his right mind would give up his place at the center of the universe? Compassion is scary. If you open up too much to people, they have the power to make you do things for them. Better to keep them at a distance, keep them on the other side of the footlights. Learn to juggle — learn to fall down in funny ways. Keep them as an audience where you can be in control. Keep the curtain up, keep the play going. It holds off judgment. See me up here? You love me, right? I'm the best, right? But if I wanted really to act, I was going to have to find the doorway to compassion, and that would be an even harder one to walk through than the door [of the *M*A*S*H* set]."[3]

Throughout his Gospel, Mark portrays Jesus as being uncomfortable with his growing renown as a miracle worker and healer. But what drives Jesus is the same compassion that Alan Alda discovered in the craft of acting: compassion that uncovers the basic humanity we all share; compassion that knocks down the walls of self and enables us to realize our connection to all God's children; compassion that enables us to open our hearts to others, to see one another as more than just the labels and numbers we assign to one another; compassion that makes us not only feel the pain of others but compels us to seek to heal that pain.

The Jesus in Mark's Gospel becomes increasingly uncomfortable with his growing renown as a miracle worker. He clearly values time away from the crowds to be alone to pray — even though that time is cut short by the needs of those around him. Jesus works miracles not out of any need of his own for the adulation of the masses but out of an extraordinary sense of compassion, a deep love for his brothers and sisters, especially those in crisis or pain. The miracles he works are not to solicit acclaim for himself but to awaken faith and trust in the Word of God, to restore in humankind God's vision of a world united as brothers and sisters under his providence ("for this purpose I have come"). Jesus' compassion for those who come to him breaks down stereotypes and defenses that divide, segregate and marginalize people; his ministry is not to restore bodies to health but to restore spirits to wholeness.

Like Jesus' rising before dawn and going to a deserted place, we too need that "deserted," "out of the way" place to re-connect with God, to rediscover God's presence in our life, to find within ourselves again a sense of gratitude for the blessings of that presence.

In imitating Christ's compassion, may we work "miracles" of charity and generosity through which our families and communities may be restored to hope and trust in the God who loves us.

May your Spirit of compassion, O Lord,
enable us to perform our own "miracles"
in our own houses and villages.
Inspired by your humility and selflessness,
may we find our joy
in lifting up the fallen,
caring for the sick,
and healing the broken-hearted.

Sixth Sunday of the Year /
Sixth Sunday after Epiphany

A leper came to Jesus and kneeling down begged him and said, "If you wish, you can make me clean." Moved with pity, Jesus stretched out his hand, touched him, and said to him, "I do will it. Be made clean."

Mark 1: 40–45

Lepers, statistics and ghosts

A writer who was laid off by his magazine in a cost-cutting move reflects on his "life as a statistic":

"I was watching the television news recently when it suddenly hit me that I was on it. Not that you'd have noticed. I was one of the 10,080,000 counted as unemployed … placing me among 6.5 percent of the non-farm workforce, the highest jobless rate in 14 years … Now I'm not looking for any sympathy, although I still don't understand why the government didn't deem the magazine that laid me off too big to fail, as it did some financial institutions … I'm sure that many of the unemployed are worse off than I am. Thanks to savings and my wife's job, we can still pay the bills.

"It's more of the psychic impact that's taking its toll: the feeling, most noticeable from 8 A.M. Monday to 5 P.M. Friday, that I'm on the outside, while everyone else — or 93.5 percent of them, anyway — is on the inside.

"And not a single one of them is returning phone calls or e-mail.

"When you're on the outside, you quickly forget what it's like on the inside. Instead of dreading a blinking light on your answering machine, you're looking forward to it. Instead of unread messages piling up in your in-box, they're trickling in. Even the Nigerian bankers have struck me from their list.

"Initially I was a bit choosy about which job postings I'd respond to, blithely assuming that employers would be stampeding for my services. Now I answer them all. I figure a bolt of lightning would find me more attractive than a prospective employer. Actually, I shouldn't say that. Several people have responded. But I think they're only teasing me. They get my hopes up with a phone call or even an interview, only to, well, forget I existed.

"After I lost my job, I turned into merely a number. Then worse: I became a ghost."[4]

We sometimes reduce others to mere statistics that serve as warnings to us of the disaster that can befall us if we aren't careful and on guard — we forget that hidden in these cold numbers are real, live people whom we have consigned to the margins because of the "uncleanliness" of their failure and misfortune. They are the "lepers" of our own time and place.

The cleansing of the leper is a climactic moment in Mark's Gospel. By just touching the leper Jesus challenges one of the strictest proscriptions in Jewish society (today's first reading in the Roman lectionary — Leviticus 13: 1–2, 44–46 — provides the context for understanding the social and religious revulsion of lepers). The leper is one of the heroic characters of Mark's Gospel (along with such figures as the poor widow who gives her only penny to the temple and the blind Bartimaeus). The leper places his entire trust in Jesus. For him, there is no doubt: this Jesus is the Messiah of hope, the Lord of life. His request for healing is more than a cry for help — it is a profession of faith: "You can make me clean."

Jesus' curing of the leper shocked those who witnessed it. Jesus did not drive the leper away, as would be the norm (the leper, according to the Mosaic Law, had no right to even address Jesus); instead, Jesus stretched out his hand and touched him. Jesus did not see an unclean leper but a human soul in desperate need.

Consider what Jesus does after healing the leper. He sends the cleansed leper to show himself to the priest "and offer for your cure what Moses prescribed." This leper's healing is a message for the Jewish establishment, represented by the priest: that the Messiah has come and is present among you.

Christ who healed the leper and the unclean comes now to "cleanse" us of our debilitating sense of self that blinds us to the sacredness and dignity of those we reject as "lepers," to heal us of our own discouragement and hopelessness so that we realize again that God extends his compassion and grace even to the likes of us.   Before God, no one is a leper beyond the reach of God's mercy and compassion; all of us are sons and daughters of the Father, made in the sacred image of the God of justice, peace and reconciliation. These especially difficult times challenge us not to let our fears or prejudices reduce people to statistical "lepers" but to reach out to one another with compassionate dignity and respectful generosity.

Jesus works his wonders not to solicit acclaim for himself but to awaken faith in God's providence, to restore God's vision of a world where humanity is united as brothers and sisters in the love of God — and not patronize them as "mission projects." Jesus calls us who would be his disciples to let our own "miracles" of charity and mercy, of forgiveness and justice, be "proof" of our committed discipleship to the Gospel and our trust in the God who is the real worker of wonders in our midst.

*S*aving God,
in your compassion we are made whole;
in your mercy we are restored to joy.
Illuminate our hearts
that we may not see others as lepers
but welcome them as sisters and brothers
    in you.
In the love and care we extend to others,
let others see your love and care
through which we have been made
    "clean" and "whole."

> "Which is easier, to say to the paralytic, 'Your sins are forgiven,' or to say, 'Rise, pick up your mat and walk?'"

Mark 2: 1–12

Not all history majors are created equal …

*T*he professor assigned to his U.S. history seminar a ten-page research paper on Thomas Jefferson, due at the end of the semester.

One student went to work that very night. School work did not come easily to him; he had to work hard to keep up. He was a history major and his dream was to be a high school history teacher. Over the next few weeks he spent hours reading, making notes and rewriting his draft. He got a C for the paper. Disappointed, the student made an appointment to meet with the professor. The professor showed him both the strengths and weaknesses of the paper, where his analysis was faulty, what facts he failed to grasp. The student rewrote the paper and got his grade up to a B-plus.

Another student in the course was a member of a fraternity. One of the great perks of membership in the frat was access to an impressive archive of research papers written by students over the years, so the second student took a couple of papers on Jefferson, cut and pasted as needed, and submitted the paper. His grade: A-minus.

Now, the obvious moral here is that the first student learned more from the research assignment. But the first student learned much more than Jeffersonian democracy. He learned *how* to learn, *how* to think, *how* to reason. He was willing to fail in order to succeed.

The second student got a good grade in a course he quickly forgot about.

The experience of the two students mirrors the point of today's Gospel. With the help of his generous and compassionate friends, a paralyzed man comes to Jesus to be healed — but instead, Jesus (to the outrage of those who witness the event) forgives the paralytic his sins. Feeling better is the "easy A"; but to heal the brokenness of the soul and spirit, to treat the illness of our own sin and self-centeredness, to mend torn relationships, is to actually "write the paper," and in the process become fully alive, fully human as God has made us to be. To be able to "pick up our mats" and walk is one thing — but God has called us to live in the light of his compassion and grace, regardless of our physical and mental abilities or limitations. Faith challenges us not to be satisfied with easy grades and merely feeling better but to take on the hard work of learning and seeking the wholeness of our souls and spirits.

Today's Gospel reading is the first of six episodes in Mark's Gospel in which Jesus and his teachings become the center of controversy. The popular Wonder-worker becomes a threat to the leadership and stature of the Pharisees and scribes.

The paralyzed man becomes — both literally and figuratively — the center of the first controversy. Jesus again makes the point that he comes not to heal bodies but to heal spirits, to restore the relationship between God and humankind, to mend the brokenness and estrangement afflicting the people of God.

The physical miracles worked by Jesus validate his Gospel of compassion and love and prefigures the great Easter miracle of God's reign to come. The paralyzed man, therefore, is first offered forgiveness by Jesus. The legalistic, tradition-bound scribes and Pharisees protest that only God can forgive sins. Exactly, Jesus says. And to emphasize the sacred mandate he has received, Jesus orders the paralytic to "pick up your mat and walk."

The four friends who help the paralyzed man meet Jesus are among the unknown saints of the Gospel. Consider the logistics: First, they had to carry their friend on a stretcher and maneuver their way through the unyielding crowds who wanted to see Jesus. When that wasn't going to work, they devised a bold plan: they carefully hoisted their friend up on the roof of the house (probably up a flight of stairs outside the building, typical of homes of Palestinian houses of the time), push aside the thatch and tiles, and lowered down their friend on his pallet, ever so carefully and gently, before Jesus. It must have been quite a sight, greeted probably, at first, with stunned silence by the crowds, then by vehement protests at this man's bypassing the crowds. But his friends would not be dissuaded.

Such extraordinary love for another human being. Jesus could not have healed the paralyzed man if the man's friends — the "roofers" — had not been part of it. Concern for their friend and confidence in Jesus' compassion compelled them to put all their ingenuity and muscle into bringing their paralyzed friend to Jesus the healer.

The "roofers" of today's gospel teach us today what friendship — Christ-like friendship — is all about: "Roofer" friends do not get stuck in self-interest and status but find joy in lifting up one another. "Roofer" friends are the first to pick up another's mat and carry their friend when he or she is wounded and broken — and they never have to be asked. "Roofer" friends readily offer all that they have and whatever they have — and "roofer" friends readily accept those gifts from one another joyfully and gratefully. "Roofer" friends stand with one another at both their crosses and resurrections.

*C*ompassionate God,
may we seek not just to feel better
but to be healed of the fears and despair,
the selfishness and arrogance
that paralyze us from living lives
    of fulfillment and purpose.
Break the strangulation of sin in our lives
and raise us from the paralysis that deadens us
    to the love and joy of your presence.

Give us the faith of the "roofers," O God,
that we may be sources of comfort and support,
    understanding and forgiveness for others.
And may we discover, in the gift of our friends,
    the blessings of your grace.

People came to Jesus and objected, "Why do the disciples of John and the disciples of the Pharisees fast, but your disciples do not fast?"
Jesus answered them, "Can the wedding guests fast while the bridegroom is with them?"

Mark 2: 18–22
[Common lectionary: Mark 2: 13–22]

All the last times

*M*ost expectant and new parents collect memories of their child's first years in one of those "Our Baby's First ... " books — Baby's first smile, Baby's first steps, Baby's first words.

But one mother believes that there should be another book: *The Book of Lasts.* It would keep track of the moments we don't realize are precious until they're gone. For example, she remembers the morning her daughter Anne crawled into bed with her and husband.

"A short time later, I woke up wedged between my husband and Anne's excess of elbows. I got out of bed, slid my arms beneath Anne and tried to lift her. No go. The little girl I used to bounce in my arms was gone. On a day I don't remember, I had carried Anne for the last time. When I set her down, I didn't know it would be forever.

"Another 'last' was when my little boy, Roman, fresh from a bath, said *Warm me up, Mommy,* and I folded by arms in a terry-cloth hug around a pink and steaming toddler. This was a daily post-bath ritual until one day when he toweled himself off and dashed to his bedroom before anyone could see his Scooby-Doo underwear."

Also missed was the last picture of Mom and Dad drawn by the kids in the style of young artists — no neck or torso, just crayoned sticks for arms and legs shooting out of a giant potato head. "If I had only known, I might have framed the last drawing, or left it hanging on the refrigerator door a while longer."[5]

Today's moments are just that — today's. In trying to check off as many of the items on our task-saturated daily "to do" lists, we overlook the moments of grace, the revelations of God's love, in the midst of our homes and workplaces and schools. In today's gospel, Jesus urges us to live to the fullest those moments in which he is present in the love of others, to cherish those experiences in which the "Bridegroom" Christ is with us in times of joy, discovery, and wonder.

Throughout Scripture, the covenant to which God calls Israel is compared to the love of husband and wife, that special intimacy experienced by the "espoused" (today's first reading from Hosea is an example). The images of the bridegroom and wedding feast that Jesus uses in today's Gospel resonated with his hearers. But the implication that he is the Bridegroom widened the growing gulf between Jesus and the Jewish establishment.

In Jesus' time, faithful Jews fasted twice a week; the Law stipulated, however, that wedding receptions were exceptions to the fast. Jesus justifies his words regarding fasting under this exception: with the Messiah's presence among them, God's promised "wedding banquet" has begun.

Jesus indicts the Pharisees' practice of fasting because it was often an act devoid of praise; it was often merely an ostentatious display of religiosity, a "badge of honor" identifying themselves as the "separated" (the meaning of the word *Pharisee*). Jesus' point (a point the Pharisees cannot grasp) is that any ritual or pietistic practice must come from the heart; it must be grounded in that special love God calls us to embrace, a love that transcends that of stipulated law and contracts and consumes one totally (like that special love between spouses completely and wholly in love).

The images of the patched cloak and the new wine in old wineskins speak to that point: in Christ, God calls us to a new attitude and a renewed spirit of intimate relationship with him that cannot be confined or diminished by the legalistic religiosity adhered to by the Pharisees.

Christ comes to re-infuse the dusty legalisms and empty rituals of the Mosaic Law with the Spirit of love and thanksgiving for all that God has done for us. The values on which we center our lives are the substance of our faith. Prayer formulas, rituals, liturgies and traditions that are truly holy express and celebrate the substance of that faith we profess.

May our vision and perception be cut from "new cloth" — a new understanding of God and the things of God because of our encounter with the Gospel Jesus.

Today Gospel reading in the Common lectionary begins with Jesus' call of Levi, "sitting at the customs post," to join his company. Levi is a tax collector — a profession that Jews considered traitorous. In the Roman governing system, individuals would "bid" for the right to collect taxes in a certain territory. The individual appointed would guarantee the amount of taxes Rome considered the area should yield; the tax collector would then collect the "taxes" in whatever amounts — and employing whatever methods — he chose, keeping as his profit whatever he collected over and above Rome's due. Jews despised tax collectors as collaborators with their Roman occupiers in the subjugation of their people. Jesus' calling of Levi — and then going to his house — further scandalizes the Pharisees. But Jesus responds that the whole reason of his ministry is to reconcile all of humanity — including and especially "sinners" — to the Father.

*L*ord Jesus,
the Bridegroom of God's wedding feast,
give us the vision of faith and charity of heart
to recognize your presence among us
and to see your face in one another.
May we honor you in our compassion and love
    for each other:
in our washing one another's feet,
in helping each other bear our crosses
    of sorrow and pain,
in lifting one another up from our tombs
    of hopelessness and despair.
May your presence among us be the light
that guides us at last to your wedding banquet
    in the kingdom of the Father.

Sunday 9 / Proper 4

"The Sabbath was made for man, not man for the Sabbath."

Mark 2: 23 — 3: 6

A cathedral of time

You are standing before one of the great cathedrals of Europe. You pass through the giant doors and enter the great nave of magnificent stained glass windows. The beautiful icons, sculptures and works of art take your breath away. The stillness transports you from the noisy, busy world outside to an entirely different place and time. You sense that you are at the threshold of God's dwelling place.

For the faithful Jew, the Sabbath observance possesses the same wonder and sense of holiness that we experience in such sacred places. The great Jewish theologian Abraham Joshua Henschl wrote that Judaism is "a religion of time aiming at the sanctification of time. The Sabbaths are our great cathedrals; and our Holy of Holies is a shrine that neither the Romans nor the Germans were able to burn."

The idea of "sacred time" is something very much at odds with our contemporary "24–7" approach to life — "keeping the Sabbath" is a quaint custom from a time long ago. With our modern sensibilities, we can't imagine a day dedicated for "not" doing anything. We've got too much to do.

But the Sabbath is not a day of prohibitions and restrictions; it is a day of privileges and freedom. Rabbi Naomi Levy writes in *To Begin Again: The Journey Toward Comfort, Strength, and Faith is Difficult Times:*

"Imagine what it might feel like to stop spending money, to stop looking to the outside world as a source of entertainment and distraction. A day of rest gives us the opportunity to find true relaxation from within ... How would our lives change if for one day each week we were to leave the world of materialism and technology and enter into the world of spirituality, nature and beauty?

"Picture a day that we spend not by fretting about the past or by worrying about the future, but by living in the sacred present. A day in which we can be still, still enough to actually hear the things we so often miss: the silent yearning of our souls which we usually deny or ignore. A day to be still enough to actually hear the things we so often ignore. A day to be still enough to hear what it is that the people in our lives are really trying to say to us. Still enough to appreciate all the gifts and blessings that we take for granted each day, still enough to feel God's presence in our lives. Imagine what it might be like to let go of all the cares of the week, to allow our bodies and souls to relax, to welcome in the peace and the joy and the holiness and the light of true rest."

The observance of the Sabbath is the third major dispute between Jesus and the Pharisees recorded in Mark's Gospel. The Pharisees are appalled that the disciples are pulling grain of wheat stalks as they walk along on the Sabbath. According to the Pharisees' strict observance, this seemingly innocent and mindless activity is considered work and, therefore, profaned the Sabbath. Jesus' response radically redefines the nature of the Sabbath: that even the Sabbath's proscriptions against work and play are second to acts of charity and mercy.

And to make the point, Jesus again performs a miracle. Immediately after his confrontation with the Pharisees, Jesus goes to the synagogue where he meets a man with a "shriveled hand." Strict rabbinical interpretation stipulated that "healings" could take place on the Sabbath only if a matter of life and death. The poor man here, while in great suffering, is hardly at death's door. But Jesus again emphasizes the sacredness of mercy and compassion by healing the man's hand on the Sabbath.

In this encounter, however, it is Jesus who responds angrily. The Pharisees cannot understand the profound meaning of what Jesus has done. They are too centered in themselves to rejoice in the love and mercy of God manifested before them. The tensions between Jesus and the Pharisees continue, setting the stage for his destruction.

The Sabbath is a cathedral not made of stones and glass, but of hours and minutes; it is not so much a date but an atmosphere in which we turn from the *what* of creation to the *why* of creation. Jesus invites us to embrace the sacredness of the Sabbath day not as a burden but as a gift, to enter heart and soul into the Sabbath as a special place, a sacred time that helps us appreciate the holiness of all time as a gift from God, the Giver of all life and time. The holiness of the Sabbath is kept in attitude and spirit: a realization that we have much for which to be grateful to God and that both sacred time and space should be set aside to allow ourselves to express that thanks.

The Sabbath is a concept that demands more than notation on our calendars or an hour or so set aside for "church." The Sabbath reminds us that the clock, the dollar and our egos are not our God, that we exist not for this time alone but for eternity. May we resolve to bring the attitude and perspective of the Sabbath into our lives: a special "place of stillness" within our week to celebrate the goodness of God.

*L*ord of the Sabbath,
lead us, body and soul, into your dwelling place.
May we keep the Sabbath
as a place of peace and reconciliation
in the sacred places within our homes and communities
and as a time of healing and restoration
in the sacred time we set aside
to "rest" in you
and re-discover your love in our midst.

Sunday 10 / Proper 5

When his relatives heard of this they set out to seize him, for they said, "He is out of his mind." The scribes who had come from Jerusalem said, "He is possessed by Beelzebul" and by the prince of demons he drives out demons ... "

"If a kingdom is divided against itself, that kingdom cannot stand. And if a house is divided against itself, that house will not be able to stand ... "

" ... whoever does the will of God is my brother and sister and mother."

Mark 3: 20–35

How wars really start

A nine-year-old asks his father, "Dad, how do wars start?"

"Well, son," his father began, "take World War I. That war started when Germany invaded Belgium ..."

"Just a minute," his wife interrupted. "It began when Archduke Francis Ferdinand of Austria was assassinated by a Serbian nationalist."

"Well, dear, that was the spark that ignited the fighting, but the political and economic factors leading to the war had been in place for some time."

"Yes, I know, honey, but our son asked how the war began and every history book says that World War I began with the murder of Archduke Ferdinand of Austria."

Drawing himself up with an air of superiority, the husband snapped, "Are you answering the question, or am I?"

The wife turned her back on him in a huff, stalked out of the room and slammed the door behind her.

When the dishes stopped rattling, an uneasy silence followed. The nine-year-old then broke the silence: "Dad, you don't have to say any more about how wars start. I understand now."

Wars begin long before the first shot is fired; houses collapse well before the first crack in the foundation; families fall apart long before the first slammed door. When our own needs come before the common good, when we cannot see or refuse to see things from the perspective of the other person, when the accumulation of wealth and the pursuit of status take the place of the things of God, "war" is certain to destroy the family's unity, the circle of friendship.

Such hardness of heart and self-centeredness fuel the conflict in today's Gospel. Jesus provokes two reactions from his hearers that are the antithesis to what he has said and done to this point.

First, the Jesus who calls his disciples to be a united "house" and community is dismissed by his own "house" as "out of his mind." They apologize for him and his exorbitant claims about himself and his challenging of their most cherished institutions and traditions, as they try to bring him home.

Second, the Jesus who has cast out demons and cured the sick is charged with being possessed himself. The scribes cannot grasp the single-minded dedication of Jesus to the will of God without the "filters" of their interpretations and traditions; hence, he must be an agent of Satan, the prince of demons (whatever the people of Gospel Palestine could not understand or explain were considered the work of "demons.")

Jesus comes to be a vehicle of unity among God's people, to reconcile humanity to God and to one another, to instill a deeper understanding of our sacred dignity as being made in God's image, to restore a renewed commitment to relations and belonging with one another. Christ destroys the barriers created by race, tribe, wealth and social status. He speaks of a new, united human family: the family of God. We are called, as the Church of the new covenant, to seek in every person the humanity we all share that comes from God, the Father of all and the Giver of everything that is good.

Jesus is surrounded by people who are afraid and threatened by his message. The scribes' assertion that he is "possessed" by demons masks their fear that Jesus may well be right about their self-serving beliefs and empty values. Jesus the "lunatic" comes with the crazy idea that love will triumph over hatred, that light will shatter the darkness, that life will conquer death. This "crazy" Jesus seeks to heal us of what is, in fact, our "lunacy" — the lunacy of allowing pettiness, pride, anger, prejudice and self-centeredness to alienate us from one another, the lunacy of exalting "me first" at the expense of others' basic necessities, the lunacy of constantly grabbing as much as we can as fast as we can while most people on this planet have nothing.

Jesus calls us to become "alive" in his lunatic sense of reconciliation, community and joy that compels us to always take the first step in forgiving and being forgiven; his spirit of humility that finds joy in doing good for others; his spirit of compassion that places love before all.

May your love, O Lord, be the foundation
    of our homes and families;
may your forgiveness be the walls
    that protect our loved ones
from the winds and storms that threaten
    to drive us apart;
may your peace be the roof that shields us
    from the rain and cold;
may your compassion be the hearth
    that warms our hearts all our days.

Sunday 11 / Proper 6

"The kingdom of God is as if someone would scatter seed on the ground ... It is like a mustard seed ..."

Mark 4: 26–24

'My Grandfather's Blessings'

*I*n her book *My Grandfather's Blessings: Stories of Strength, Refuge and Belonging,* physician Rachel Naomi Remen tells of the many unusual gifts she received from her beloved grandfather, an Orthodox rabbi and scholar.

When Rachel was four, her grandfather gave her a paper cup. She expected to find something special inside — but it was filled with dirt. The disappointed little girl told her grandfather that she wasn't allowed to play with dirt. Her grandfather smiled. He took her little teapot from her doll's tea set and took his granddaughter to the kitchen and filled it with water. He put the little cup on a windowsill in her room and handed her the teapot. "If you promise to put some water in this cup every day, something may happen," he told her.

This made little sense to a four-year-old, but Rachel promised. "Every day," he repeated. At first, Rachel did not mind pouring water into the cup, but as the days went on and nothing happened, it became harder and harder for the little girl to remember her promise. After a week, she asked her grandfather if it was time to stop yet. Grandfather shook his head. "Every day," he repeated.

The second week it became even harder, but Grandfather held her to her promise: "Every day." Sometimes she would only remember about the water after she went to bed and would have to get up in the middle of the night and water it in the dark. But, in the end, Rachel did not miss a single day of watering.

Then, one morning three weeks later, there were two little green leaves that had not been there the night before. Little Rachel was astonished. She could not wait to tell her grandfather, certain that he would be as surprised as she was — but, of course, he wasn't. Carefully he explained to his beloved granddaughter that life is everywhere, hidden in the most ordinary and unlikely places.

Rachel was delighted with her discovery. "And all it needs is water, Grandpa?"

Gently, he touched her on the top of her head. "No, dear Rachel. All it needs is your faithfulness."[6]

Faith is the ability to see the potential in the smallest of things and the courage and perseverance to unlock that potential. Humanity's dreams of peace, community and justice will be realized, first, in the everyday acts of such goodness of each one of us. The mustard seed — that tiny speck containing the chemical energy to create the great tree — is a natural parable for the greatness that God raises up from small beginnings.

Farming is a matter of hard work and patient faith: All the farmer can do is plant the seed and nurture it along with water and care; God's unseen hand in creation transforms the tiny seed into a great harvest. Today's Gospel parables of the sower (this particular version of the parable of the sower is unique to Mark's Gospel) and the mustard seed, then, are calls to patience, hope and readiness.

Jesus may have been directing his words to the Zealots, a Jewish sect that sought the political restoration of Israel. Many Zealots were terrorists, employing murder and insurrection to destabilize the Roman government. The Zealots looked to the coming of a Messiah who would restore the Jewish nation. Jesus, however, calls them to see their identity as God's people not in terms of political might but of interior faith and spiritual openness to the love of God.

Christ asks us to embrace the faith of the sower: to "plant" seeds of peace, reconciliation and justice wherever and whenever we can in the certain knowledge that, in God's good time, our plantings will result in the harvest of the kingdom of God. He entrusts to us, his disciples, with the work of making the reign of God a reality in our own lives with patient but determined "mustard seed faith": the conviction that, from the smallest and humblest acts of justice, kindness and compassion, the kingdom of God will take root and grow.

*I*nstill in us, O Lord,
the spirit of mustard seed faith:
despite our qualms and fears,
make us vehicles of your compassion
    for the sake of others;
despite our self-consciousness and hesitation,
make us planters of your peace, justice
    and reconciliation
in our own small corner of the Father's kingdom.

Sunday 12 / Proper 7

Jesus woke up and rebuked the wind, and said to the sea, "Quiet! Be still!"

Mark 4: 35–41

Blessed stillness

*E*very afternoon, after putting her daughter down for her nap, she lugs a chair out to the backyard and sits. Just sits. Sometimes she enjoys the antics of a chipmunk or robin, meditates on a bee hovering over the garden, or loses herself in the clouds dancing above her. After an hour or so, she returns to the diapers and toys and story books to find her little one ready to charge through the afternoon. But, thanks to her few moments of precious stillness, Mom is re-charged as well.

The morning is filled with phone calls and meetings. Like most managers, cajoling, convincing, motivating, fixing, adapting, tracking, counting, admonishing, and completing are his business. On the rare days when he can escape at lunch, he picks up a sandwich and finds a quiet place in the park or the library. He loses himself in a chapter from Thomas Merton or Henri Nouwen or soaks in every word, every image of one of the psalms. Sales figures might define him as a professional, but it is such moments of stillness that define him as a human being.

Like most teenagers, his life is filled with confusion and questions, discoveries and realizations, moodiness and angst. Sometimes the rollercoaster of being sixteen and a high school sophomore becomes too much, so he closes his door, lies on his bed, and puts on his headphones. But the music is not the usual rock that makes his parents' heads spin and eyes roll. It's a wordless CD of soft jazz or classic guitar that quiets the nerves and soothes the spirit. In music he wouldn't dare admit to his friends that he listens to, the teenager finds the sanctuary of stillness.

The words Jesus addresses to the storm can just as well be addressed to us: *Peace! Be still!* In our stormy, whirlwind lives, we need to make time intentionally for peace and stillness in order to hear the voice of the Spirit, to reset our compass as we navigate our small boats through life's stormy Galilee sea, to check our bearings to make sure that we are living our lives in the hope and joy in which God created us to live them.

The "storms" we experience in our everyday lives mirror the turbulent Galilee. The Sea of Galilee is really a land-locked lake 600 feet below sea level. Ravines in the hills and mountains surrounding the Galilee act as natural wind tunnels. In the evening, as the warm air of the day rises above the water, cool air rushes in through the ravines. The effect is amazing: the tranquil lake is whipped into a fury of white-capped six-foot waves. In the midst of this terrorizing experience, Jesus calms both the sea and his disciples' fear. The evangelist Mark is recounting this story to a terrified and persecuted community. Today's Gospel is intended to reassure them of the Risen Christ's constant presence in the storms they struggle through for the sake of their faith in his reign to come.

The wisdom and grace of the "awakened" Jesus is present to us throughout the journeys of our lives to "calm" the adversities and tragedies that either help us grow in understanding life or consume us in despair and hopelessness. Like the harried mother, the busy executive and the overwhelmed teenager, we need moments of stillness in order to retake control of our lives and realize that our lives are really in control of the Giver of life, the God of love, the Father of all that is good.

*C*ome, Lord Jesus,
and quiet the storms that batter our lives
that threaten to sink us
in waves of fear, despair and doubt.
May your peace be the route we follow;
may your compassion be the star
by which we navigate our way
on the seas of our lives.

Jairus fell at Jesus' feet and pleaded earnestly with him, saying, "My daughter is at the point of death. Please, come lay your hands on her that she may get well and live."
There was a woman afflicted with hemorrhages for twelve years. She had heard about Jesus and came up behind him in the crowd and touched his cloak. She said, "If I but touch his clothes, I shall be cured."

Mark 5: 21–43

A 'driving-purposed' life

*A*s a young woman, she prayed that God would give her a grand purpose in life.

God answered by giving her two daughters and a set of car keys. "Drive," God said.

And drive she did. In her red Ford Tempo, she drove her girls and their friends everywhere — to the mall and to volleyball practice. To softball games and the mall. To the youth group at church and the mall. To the beach. To Taco Bell. To school. To the mall.

It was either she drive them or risk them finding rides with someone's sister's boyfriend. As long as her daughters and their myriad of friends were in the backseat of her car with her at the wheel, she would know where they were.

And she loved it. It actually proved to be quite educational — she learned she could be invisible. The girls would pile into her car and start talking about stuff girls talk about, which meant boys and other girls. You can learn a lot by being invisible. During her years of driving girls, her car was used as a cafeteria, a beauty parlor, a dressing room, and sometimes as a confessional and a sanctuary.

Something amazing happened when her little red Tempo filled with girls.

God entered.

Did the girls ever realize God in the car? Sometimes, she thinks: every once in a while they would ask her a question about God, about faith, about Ouija boards, about levitating. They discussed Buddhism, paganism and Marilyn Manson. And there were times when they even prayed out loud together.

Not long ago, the mother of her daughter's childhood best friend called to thank her for what she had done for her daughter Kelly, who died from leukemia at the age of 21. Kelly's mom was thanking her for much more than providing car service for Kelly.

Now that her daughters are grown, she misses her "driving-purposed" life. It was mundane and ordinary, yet incredibly holy.[7]

Moms and Dads know that parenthood is a full-time vocation that demands everything we have and are for the sake of the children who depend on them.

Jairus, in today's Gospel, is a model of such dedicated parenthood.

Jairus was a man of considerable authority and stature in the Jewish community. Yet, for the sake of his daughter, he puts aside his pride and his instinctive distrust of an "anti-establishment" rabbi like Jesus and becomes a "beggar" for her before Jesus. Despite the ridicule of the mourners and the depth of his despair, Jesus is Jairus' hope.

A second healing story is inserted in the middle of the Jairus account. The chronically ill woman is so convinced that Jesus not only can help her but *will* help her that she fights her way through the pushing and shoving crowds just to touch the cloak of Jesus. She realizes not only the power of Jesus to heal her but the depth of his love and compassion to *want* to heal her. Her faith is rewarded.

For Mark, Jairus and the unnamed woman in today's Gospel are models of faith. Both Jairus and the woman place their hope in the love of God — God who is Father for us, his sons and daughters, God whose love heals and restores and lifts up — and that love is revealed in their midst. In the healings of Jairus' daughter and the hemorrhaging woman, Jesus shows us the life and hope we can bring into our world through the providence of God and the goodness everyone possesses.

God of all good things,
open our hearts and spirits
to behold your love in our midst.
Be our hope in times of despair;
be our healing in time of illness and hurt.
May yours be the hand
   we grasp when we fall;
May yours be the light
   that leads out of the darkness of fear
   into the light of morning peace.

"Where did this man get all this? What kind of wisdom has been given to him? What mighty deeds are wrought by his hands! Is he not the carpenter, the son of Mary ... ?"
Jesus said to them, "A prophet is not without honor except in his native place and among his own kin and in his own house."

Mark 6: 1–6

A little child shall lead

Spence is a great kid. And a gutsy one.

While still in the womb, Spence suffered a stroke. As a result, the eight-year-old has limited use of the right side of his body. Spence came home one day from school and told his parents that the other kids were beginning to talk about him and wonder why he couldn't play certain sports and games like everyone else plays. Of course, his parents were concerned — we all know how cruel kids can be about the slightest differences. So Spence and his parents went to school and talked with the teacher and principal. Spence devised a plan.

Spence got up in front of four different second-grade classrooms, faced all the kids, and told them what happened to him on his way to being born. He calmly explained how there were things he couldn't do but many other things he could do. The kids asked questions and Spence answered them all. Spence doesn't hesitate to ask for help now and his classmates are always there for him.

Spence's dad was not only proud of his son, but inspired.

"I couldn't believe his courage ... I knew there were problems in my own life I was failing to deal with. I was hiding from them. Spence showed me another way. It took a few months, but I finally mustered the courage to ask for the help I needed. Spence showed me help [and] acceptance are all around me.

"We talk about how we can be there for our kids, but sometimes they're the ones who are there for us."[8]

Spence is nothing less than a prophet — "one who proclaims." There are prophets and saints like Spence living right here among us who mirror the Jesus of the Gospel in their lives of quiet integrity and generosity. Taking on the role of prophet begins with the integrity to confront who we are, the wisdom to realize the gulf that often exists between the values we profess and the values we actually live, and the courage to re-create our place in the world in the justice and mercy of God.

But such "prophecy" often goes unnoticed, if not outright rejected. Today's Gospel introduces a new theme in Mark's Gospel: the blindness of people to the power and authority of Jesus. The people of Jesus' own hometown reject his message. They consider Jesus too much "one of them" to be taken seriously. They are too obsessed with superficialities — occupation, ancestry, origins — to realize God present in their midst and to be affected by that presence.

The authority that Jesus' hearers sense in him is an authority and wisdom that transcends office, title and economic power; it is an authority rooted in wisdom that comes from experience and a lived commitment to do what is right and just. Jesus' authority is not derived from his ability to manipulate the fears, suspicions, apathy and ignorance of those around him but from the spirit of mercy, justice and compassion he is able to call forth from them.

There are prophets and saints like Spence living right here among us. In their lives of quiet integrity, courage and generosity, they mirror the Jesus of the Gospel. In embracing discipleship, we take on that same role of prophet. To "proclaim" the Word we have heard can result in our being ostracized, ridiculed, rejected and isolated — but genuine faith never falters in the conviction that the justice of God will triumph over injustice, that his mercy will triumph over hatred, that his light will triumph over the darkness of sin and death.

O God, wellspring of compassion,
make us prophets of your compassion.
Inspired by your wisdom and grace,
may our smallest attempts to forgive,
    to console, to help,
reveal your presence in our midst.
May our perseverance to live lives
    of justice and integrity
proclaim within our own places and communities
your Son's Gospel of reconciliation and peace.

Sunday 15

Jesus summoned the Twelve and began to send them out two by two and gave them authority over unclean spirits. He instructed them to take nothing for their journey but a walking stick ... The Twelve drove out many demons, and they anointed with oil many who were sick and cured them.

Mark 6: 7–13
[Roman lectionary]

Walking sticks

She begins her program with Bach's *Jesu, Joy of Man's Desiring*. Her fingers dance over the frets of her guitar with the quiet confidence of her years of practice and study. She next plays an Irish air, then a Bob Dylan folk song and finally a jazz improvisation of her own creation. She performs for an audience of one: a 70-year-old woman dying of cancer. The venue: the dying woman's room at the local hospice. Music is her ministry, providing a measure of peace and tranquility for those taking the last steps from this world into eternity.

Most spring and summer nights, as soon as he gets home from the office, he heads to his small garden behind the garage. This quarter-acre is his favorite place on earth. He grows tomatoes, beans and corn. He saves a few things for his own family; he shares the rest of the harvest of the good earth with needy families served by the local soup kitchen and pantry.

She suffered from bulimia as a teenager. Thanks to her wise and caring family, she overcame this devastating disease. Now a mother herself, she read about a support group for girls suffering from eating disorders. Every week she is there. She says very little; she is present to listen and to support, and when asked one-on-one by a girl who is terrified at what is happening to her, she offers the hope of her own story.

With their "walking sticks" — guitars, vegetable seeds, and their own stories and experiences — these three and so many others like them realize that Christ has sent them forth, like the Twelve in today's Gospel, to be his prophets of peace, apostles of compassion, ministers of healing.

In today's Gospel, the Twelve — each of whom has been called personally by Jesus — are given the title of *apostle* — "one who is sent." These unlikely candidates for such a task are carefully prepared and taught by Jesus for this moment. They undertake their first preaching and healing tour depending only on God for their inspiration and on the charity of others for their needs — remember that hospitality was considered a sacred responsibility in the east: it was not up to the stranger to seek hospitality but up to the prospective host to offer it. Jesus instructs his missioners to "travel light" — to focus on the journey and the ministry with which they have been entrusted, not with accumulating wealth, status and power.

Aware of God's love in our own lives, we are called to bring that love into the lives of others in a spirit of humility and gratitude. As we make our own journey to the reign of God, may we heal the broken and help the stumbling we meet along our way in faithfulness to the God who heals us and helps us up when we stumble and fall; may each step of our life's journey be a moment of grace, of encounter with the holy, of rebirth and transformation, of healing.

*W*ith our walking sticks of generosity
and our tunics of humility,
may we journey forth as your messengers,
Christ Jesus.
May we be your ministers of peace,
vehicles of your reconciliation,
and servants of your justice
in every house we enter.

Proper 10

The death of John the Baptizer: Herod had sent men who arrested John, bound him in prison on account of Herodias, his brother Philip's wife, because Herod had married her. For John had been telling Herod, "It is not lawful for you to have your brother's wife."

Mark 6: 14–29
[Common lectionary]

Reading your own death warrant

*I*magine reading your name on a hit list.

That's exactly what happened to Shirin Ebadi. Ms. Ebadi is a human rights lawyer and activist in Iran. In her book, *Iran Awakening: A Memoir of Revolution and Hope*, Ms. Ebadi, who was awarded the 2003 Nobel Peace Prize for her work, remembers the nightmarish discovery:

In the fall of 2000, the government of Iran admitted complicity in dozens of murders of teachers, journalists and other intellectuals deemed to be enemies of the Islamic state. Ms. Ebadi represented the family of two victims, a husband and wife. The judge granted Ms. Ebadi and the lawyers for other victims just ten days to read the thousands of pages in government files in order to prepare their cases. The stakes could not have been higher: This was the first time that the Iranian government had acknowledged that it had murdered its critics. A rogue death squad within the Ministry of Intelligence was believed responsible. The perpetrators would finally be held accountable.

Ms. Ebadi and the other lawyers arrived at the courthouse at the appointed time to review the files. After dividing up the cartons of material, they began to read the details of the brutal murders buried in the stacks of bureaucratic files. Ms. Ebadi remembers:

"I had reached a page more detailed, and more narrative, than any previous section, and I slowed down to focus. It was the transcript of a conversation between a government minister and a member of the death squad. When my eyes first fell on the sentence that would haunt me for years to come, I thought I had misread. I blinked once, but it stared back at me from the page: *The next person to be killed is Shirin Ebadi. Me.*

"My throat went dry. I read the line over and over again, the printed words blurring before me ... My would-be assassin [went to] the minister of intelligence, requesting permission to carry out my killing. Not during the month of Ramadan [the holy month of prayer and fasting, in Islam], the minister replied. But they don't fast anyway, the mercenary had argued; these people are divorced from God. It was through this belief — that the intellectuals, that I, had abandoned God — that they justified the killings as a religious duty.

"I remember mostly an overwhelming disbelief. Why do they hate me so much? I wondered. What have I done to elicit hate of this order? How have I created enemies so eager to spill my blood that they cannot wait for Ramadan to end? We didn't stop to talk about it then; there was no time for gasps or sympathetic murmurings of *How awful that you were next on the list.* We couldn't waste any of our limited, precious time with the files. I sipped my tea and went on, though my fingers felt paralyzed and I turned the papers with difficulty. At around two o'clock we finished, and it was only then that I told the other lawyers, as we passed through the courtyard outside. They shook their heads, murmured *Alhamdolellah,* thanks to God; unlike the victims whose families we were defending, I had evaded death."[9]

Today we read, outside of Jesus' own death, one of the most horrific stories in the Gospels. Between Jesus' sending off the Twelve on their first missionary journey and their return, Mark inserts the story of John the Baptizer's execution. At first, this narrative seems out of place — but its inclusion here serves as an important benchmark for understanding the meaning of discipleship and the resurrection.

The works that Jesus and the Twelve are performing have reached the ears of King Herod himself. Rumors have been circulating that the Baptizer has been raised from the dead. Mark recounts the details of John's martyrdom and burial to make clear that a new chapter of human history begins in Jesus, that God has set in motion a re-creation of humanity in Jesus, that the long-awaited but little understood reign of God has begun. John is the precursor of the Christ event, not the event himself.

In Mark's Gospel, John's death foreshadows the death of Jesus (just as John's appearance at the beginning of the Gospel sets the stage for Jesus' coming on the scene). As John pays the ultimate price for speaking truth to power, Jesus will give his life for the Gospel he has preached. A similar convergence of fear, cowardice, hatred and manipulation that leads to John's beheading will end in Jesus' crucifixion.

We often react to the Baptizers in our midst as Herod does: We know in our deepest being that they speak wisdom and justice and we desperately want to embrace it in our lives — but when their words become too demanding and too challenging, when they require a conversion of us that is well beyond our comfort zone, when their call subjects us to ridicule or isolation, then we find some way to justify doing away with them. Authentic faith, belief that means anything, requires the would-be disciple of Jesus to live the Word we have heard and seen, regardless of the cost.

Both the story of John's death and Shirin Ebad's targeting for execution show that there is a price to be paid for speaking truth to power. Ridicule, isolation, rejection — even death — can be required of everyone and anyone — us included — for taking seriously God's call to be his prophets: to proclaim God's compassion, forgiveness and justice in times and places that are in determined opposition to the very idea of those things.

But God promises a place of honor in his kingdom to come to those like John and Shirin who dare to speak his word of justice and righteousness. May their example inspire us to take on, with their integrity and conviction, the role of prophet of the God of life and love.

God of steadfast love,
may your Spirit inspire us with integrity and conviction
to take on the work of being
    your prophets and apostles.
Instill in us the fire of that love
that we may proclaim
in our own Jerusalems and Nazareths
the coming of your kingdom of justice and peace.

Sunday 16 / Proper 11

"Come away by yourselves to a deserted place and rest a while."

Jesus' heart was moved with pity for the vast crowd, for they were like sheep without a shepherd.

Mark 6: 30–34
Mark 6: 30–34, 53–56

Psalm 23 distorted

*H*e knew the numbers. He was never without his Blackberry nor did he venture too far away from the business cable channels. And when he wasn't reading the numbers, he was studying the reasons behind them and the prospects for new and higher numbers. *My family's security* was his mantra — but as he obsessed about the numbers in his portfolio, his wife and children were becoming strangers. The numbers he thought secured his life have *become* his life.

My shepherd is the stock market ticker, there is nothing else that matters …

She is devastated. She had been done in, cheated, abused. Her hurt has hardened into anger. A shell seems to have formed around her. She trusts no one. She wallows in self-pity. She vows revenge. What he had done to her was despicable, there was no question of that — but what her anger is doing to her now is crippling.

Anger and emotion are my shepherds, they lead me along the path of isolation and vengeance …

They are dedicated to the "cause." Whatever is required, they give it their all. They are true believers. The cause becomes the focus of their lives. They have little tolerance for those who don't grasp or appreciate the issues involved — and even less for those who dare disagree with them. While their cause is noble and just, their zeal isolates them and creates a whole new source of pain and alienation far more divisive and unjust as the "cause."

The cause is my shepherd, I am blind to anything else ...

"Stage mothers" are not just the stuff of show business legend. "Stage mothers" — and "stage fathers" — are found in every place and in every field of endeavor. There are "stage" parents pushing, pushing, pushing their children to excel in everything from softball to spelling bees. They obsess over the child's progress on the soccer field, the science fair, the pageant runway. These sad parents are so driven to make their children's future a success that they miss the beauty and wonder of their present childhood.

My shepherd is my obsession, leading me to disappointing fields of fame and fortune ...

Truth be told, the real "shepherds" we follow are often balance sheets, emotions that take control of our lives, and whatever even remotely promises a life of celebrity and wealth. We seek affirmation, reassurance, self-respect, support and approval from a fail-safe, formula shepherd. We are, in fact, the "shepherdless" for whom Jesus' heart breaks in today's Gospel.

As today's pericope from Mark begins, the apostles return from their first mission of preaching and healing and report to Jesus. He gathers them in a "deserted" place, but the people find them and keep coming. Even their attempt to escape by boat to the other side of the lake is foiled once word gets out. This incident (which precedes his account of the feeding of the multitude — next Sunday's Gospel in the Roman lectionary) offers two important insights into our Church's ministry: that the mission of the Church does not spring from mass marketing techniques or publicity strategies but from the Gospel of compassion we seek to live and share, from the authority of our commitment to forgiveness and reconciliation; and that leadership, inspired by the wisdom of God, means not dictating and ruling over others but inspiring, providing for and selflessly caring for those whom we are called to lead.

In Christ Jesus, God has raised up for us a shepherd to lead us in our search, not for the empty riches of consumerism, but for the priceless treasures of compassion and reconciliation; a shepherd to guide us in negotiating life's rough crags and dangerous drop-offs to make our way to God's pasture of peace and fulfillment; a shepherd who journeys with us and helps us clear the obstacles and hurdles of fear and self-interest to live lives centered in what is right and just.

This Sunday's Gospel reading in the Common lectionary concludes with the final verses of Mark 6 (verses 53–54) in which Jesus continues his healing ministry in the region of Gennesaret. The verses underscore the growing popularity of Jesus as teacher and healer.

*O*pen our hearts and consciences,
Christ our shepherd,
that we may hear your voice of compassion and justice
calling us to establish your Father's reign
in our own time and place.

Sunday 17 / Proper 12

"There is a boy here who has five barley loaves and two fish; but what good are these for so many?"

John 6: 1–15

A PBJ blessed and broken for you

*W*hile the kids are getting dressed for school, Mom is in the kitchen making their lunches. Katie likes her sandwiches cut in quarters; Bobby prefers strawberry jam. As she packs the sandwiches, she smiles, imagining the delighted look on their faces when they open the dessert treats she places in the bag. What she is doing is a *sacrament* of a kind: With peanut butter and jelly, apple slices and cupcakes, the love of God embraces them all in their mother's care.

A few days before Christmas, the kids take over the kitchen to make Christmas cookies. Mom is there too, more to protect her kitchen than to supervise the baking. Frankly, the cookies that result are anything but spectacular — the reindeer-shaped cookies look more like fat cocker spaniels, the Santa cookies bear no ready resemblance to the jolly old elf, and the red and green sparkles are *piled on* rather than "sprinkled." But the kids have a ball — and are making memories that they will treasure long after they celebrate this same messy *sacrament* with their own children.

Her heart is breaking for her friend and all that she and her family have had to endure: the diagnosis, the difficult surgery, the chemotherapy, the precarious future. All she can do for her friend is pray — and make lasagna. And so she does. Three times a week she takes her turn making supper for her friend and her family. The food that she and the other friends prepare is nothing less than *sacrament* — compassion and concern made real in cheese and meat sauce.

A sacrament, St. Augustine said, is the visible sign of God's invisible grace. The gifts we give to one another are sacramental when they manifest the love and mercy of God; they are Eucharistic when they transform us and others as a community bound by that love. In our sharing of the body of Christ, may we become the body of Christ for one another, making the limitless, complete love of Christ real for all.

Today the lectionary interrupts the semi-continuous readings from Mark's Gospel for a five-week reading of Chapter 6 from the Gospel of John — the "bread of life" discourse of Jesus. While Jesus' institution of the Eucharist is the focus of the Last Supper accounts in the three synoptic Gospels, John's narrative of the Last Supper centers on Jesus' washing the feet of his disciples (in John's Gospel, the Last Supper is not a Passover meal; John writes that Jesus dies on the *preparation* day for Passover). Chapter 6 is John's Eucharistic theology.

The "bread of life" discourse is introduced by the miracle of the feeding of the multitude with a few loaves and fish — the only miracle of Jesus recorded in all four Gospels. This story was cherished by the first Christians for whom the Eucharist was becoming the center of their life together. Jesus' actions are indeed "Eucharistic": bread (and fish) are given, Jesus gives thanks (the word used in the Greek text of Mark's Gospel is *eucharisteo*), breaks the bread and the community feasts.

The multiplication of the loaves and fish did not start with nothing; Jesus was able to feed the crowds because a little boy was willing to share all he had; from his gift, small though it was, Jesus worked a miracle — and a new community of faith was formed as a result. Eucharist is possible only when self defers to community, only when serving others is exalted over being served, only when differences dissolve and the common and shared are honored above all else.

We are called by Christ to become the Eucharist we receive at this altar: giving thanks for what we have received by sharing those gifts — our talents, our riches, ourselves — to work our own miracles of creating communities of joyful faith.

*L*ord Jesus,
you give us your life and love
in the bread and wine of the Eucharist.
May we become what we receive at your table:
make us a sacrament of your compassion and peace
for our hurting and broken world.

Sunday 18 / Proper 13

"Do not work for food that perishes but for the food that endures for eternal life … "

John 6: 24–35

'Up'

*T*he animated film *Up,* from the creative wizards at Pixar, begins with one of the most touching and poetic four minutes ever seen in the movies — all told without a word of dialogue.

A quiet, shy kid named Carl meets Ellie, a real spitfire. They both dream of being explorers, of going on great adventures to faraway places. Ellie and Carl grow up, fall in love, marry, transform a ramshackle house into their dream home. They save their loose change in a glass jug for their dream trip to South America — but real life gets in the way: work, home and car repairs, medical bills. But they are happy. And in an instant, they are celebrating their fiftieth wedding anniversary. Soon after, Ellie succumbs to cancer, leaving the grieving Carl lost and alone.

After Ellie is gone, Carl finds "My Adventure Book," the scrapbook Ellie kept since they were children. The first pages are filled with the silly, funny little treasures and memories of childhood. Then there is a page Ellie has labeled "Stuff I'm Going To Do." On these pages Ellie planned to chronicle their South American adventure. Carl is stung with remorse that he never kept his promise to Ellie to take her on such a trip. But as Carl turns the page, he sees that Ellie has collected pictures of their life together — their wedding, working side by side on their house, the simple joys of going out for ice cream together. Under one of the last pictures taken of the two together, Ellie has written: *Carl, Thanks for the great adventure — Go and have a new one! Love, Ellie.*

Carl realizes that he and Ellie have indeed shared a great adventure: they dreamed together, faced and survived crushing disappointments together, grew happily old together.

Love and friendship are life's great adventure.

Carl and Ellie discover that life does not have to be exotic and exhilarating to be lived to the fullest. A life of true joy and meaning is driven not by "perishable" material things and fleeting experiences but by the "nonperishable" values of God.

In today's pericope from John's "bread of life" discourse (chapter 6), Jesus is apparently speaking to two groups : those who witnessed the miracle of the loaves (last Sunday's Gospel in the Roman lectionary) and those who did not see the miracle but have heard about it and demand to see a similar sign. To the former, Jesus tells them that there is something much deeper in this event than "perishable food" being multiplied; the real "food" is the word of God proclaimed, its power and authority manifested in the miracles of the loaves. To the latter group who seek a sign as the Israelites sought a sign from Moses, Jesus reminds them that it was not Moses himself but God working through Moses that provided their "grumbling" Exodus ancestors with bread in the desert (recalled in today's first reading from Exodus). God has given his people new bread for the new covenant — the Risen Christ.

The most difficult challenge of our time is to accomplish the "work" of God while "working" to establish and succeed in our careers, to make a place in our homes and hearts for the "bread" that is Christ amid the "fast food" being shoved in our faces from every direction. May God give us the wisdom to live lives grounded in the "food that endures" beyond the fleeting and the perishable, the "bread" of God that feeds and nurtures us for our own "great adventure" to the dwelling place of the Father.

*F*eed our souls, O Lord,
with the imperishable bread of your wisdom
and the wine of your grace,
that our lives may be the "great adventure"
of creating your enduring reign
    of compassion, justice and peace.

> "I am the living bread that came down from heaven; whoever eats this bread will live forever ...
>
> "Everyone who listens to my Father and learns from him comes to me ... whoever believes has eternal life."

John 6: 41–51

Consumed by the music

𝒮he will never forget that night. She was eight years old. She was visiting her aunt and uncle in New York. They took her to Avery Fisher Hall to hear the great flutist Jean Pierre Rampal. She was captivated by the music of the flute — at once, light and airy during a Bach concerto, then rich and exciting during a Celtic reel or Joplin rag. When she returned home, she picked up a small plastic recorder in her school's small music room. She found an instruction book in the library and holed up in her room. Before the afternoon was over, she was able to pluck out one of the melodies Rampal had played that night.

She begged her parents for lessons. They could hardly refuse. No music teacher had a more faithful student. Along the way she learned piano and had fun with a guitar, but it was the flute that was her passion. By college, she had mastered the instrument. Before she graduated, she was playing professionally. Today she is a featured performer on the flute and teaches master classes at a conservatory. But her greatest joy is when her playing lights up the music inside the soul of another eight-year-old.

We have all had experiences like this young flute virtuoso when we have been "consumed" by what we have "consumed" — the satisfaction of learning, developing an art or skill, falling in love awakens in us a passion that becomes the focus of our lives. Jesus calls us to approach the Eucharist the same way: to allow ourselves to be consumed by what we consume at this table

175

in order to become for others the bread of selfless kindness and compassionate generosity we have been given.

In much the same way that Jesus' hearers are reacting to his discourse in John 6, the Israelites whined to Moses during the trying days of the Exodus ("murmured" is the word used in Scripture): *Why did we leave Egypt? We were slaves there but at least there was food. Now we're in the middle of nowhere with nothing to eat. We're going to die out here.* So God provided Moses and his fellow travelers "manna" to eat. Scripture describes manna "as a fine, white flake-like thing." Early each day, Israelite families would gather about two quarts of manna and grind it to bake into cakes. As the sun rose higher in the sky as the day wore on, the remaining manna would evaporate.

Many scientists believe that these "flakes" were formed from honeydew secreted by a certain insect that fed on the sap of tamarisk trees (yum!). In the dry desert air, most of the moisture in the honeydew quickly evaporated, leaving sticky droplets of the stuff on plants and the ground. Since the Exodus, manna became the living symbol of God's providence and love for the Jewish people.

To the "murmuring" Jews he encounters in today's Gospel, Jesus tries to help them see the deeper meaning of his claim to be "bread come down from heaven." As in the Exodus experience, manna is the manifestation of God's providence in our midst. Manna is food for our own journeys to God — manna is generosity and kindness, consolation and support, the constant, unconditional love of family and friends. God sends us manna in many forms every day of our lives; the challenge of faith is to trust in God enough to look for manna, to collect it before it disappears, and to consume it and be consumed by it. The operative verbs in today's Gospel are "believe" and "trust": God provides for and sustains our faith in his gift of Jesus the Bread of life in the same way that First Testament wisdom nourished all who paid heed.

Christ is the "bread of heaven" that transcends this experience of life to the life of God. Christ the bread is the love, justice and compassion of God incarnate; God, our "Father," is revealed in him. To receive the Eucharist worthily, we must allow ourselves not only to consume but to be consumed by the life and love of God.

*W*ith gratitude,
we come to your table, Lord Jesus,
to feast on the bread and wine that is you.
Let us be consumed by what we consume here;
let us give to others what we receive;
let us become the sacrament of your body and blood:
that we may become "manna" for those we love
and the "bread" of your presence in our midst.

"Whoever eats my flesh and drinks my blood has eternal life, and I will raise him up on the last day."

John 6: 51–58

Foodies

*W*e all look at food differently.

For some of us, food is all about taste. Who cares about fat or sodium or sugar — if it tastes good, fine. And the bigger the serving, the better. Deep fried, better still. If it comes in a bag, a box or a six-pack, perfect. We'll work it off — right after the game. Really. As soon as we can lift ourselves off the couch. OK, maybe we'll work it off tomorrow.

Others among us take a very different approach to food. We are careful about ingredients; we seek the healthiest choices; we want to know all we can about what we put into our own bodies and what we feed our children.

Food can be our best friend. The right food comforts us, offers us refuge, reassures us. Pick your comfort food: white wine when you're tense, pizza when a deadline looms, Ben & Jerry's when the relationship ends.

But food can be the enemy — when you can't fit into the new dress or suit, when you're struggling to make your weight for the team. And the war with food can have tragic results for the young teen starving herself to look like the model on the cover of *Glamour.*

Food can also be the manifestation of love: the grandmother happily baking her grandchildren's favorite cookies, the young man spending a whole day cooking dinner to impress the new love of his life, brothers and sisters spending weeks shopping and cooking their contributions to the family's Thanksgiving feast.

Food can be little more than fuel; it can be misused and actually harm us.

Food can be an art.

But good food nourishes and sustains — and it can assure us that we are loved.

These past few Sundays we have heard a lot about food. In chapter 6 of John's Gospel, which we have been reading the past four Sundays, Jesus calls himself the "Bread of life" and, in rather graphic images, invites his hearers to "eat" his flesh and "drink" his blood.

Two dimensions of Jewish worship provide the context of today's Gospel, the fourth part of the "bread of life" discourse:

When an animal was sacrificed on the temple altar, part of the meat was given to worshipers for a feast with family and friends at which God was honored as the unseen "Guest." It was even believed by some that God entered into the flesh of the sacrificed animal, so that when people rose from the feast they believed they were literally "God-filled."

In Jewish thought, blood was considered the vessel in which life was contained: as blood drained away from a body so did its life. The Jews, therefore, considered blood sacred: blood belonged to God alone. In animal sacrifices, the blood was ritually drained from the carcass and solemnly "sprinkled" upon the altar and the worshipers by the priest as a sign of being touched directly by the "life" of God.

With this understanding, then, John summarizes his theology of the Eucharist, the new Passover banquet (remember that John's Last Supper account will center around the *mandatum*, the theology of servanthood, rather than the blessing and breaking of the bread and the sharing of the cup): To feast on Jesus the "bread" is to "feast" on the very life of God — to consume the Eucharist is to be consumed by God.

For the first Christians, Jesus' words evoked the Eucharistic supper they gathered together to eat on the first day of the week. But in calling himself "bread," in inviting us to feast on his own "body" and "blood," Jesus reminds us that it his spirit of compassion, his reflection of the Father's love, his Gospel of justice and peace that should nourish and sustain us in order to live complete and purposeful lives, to awaken our senses and focus our consciousness on seeking God and discovering his presence in our lives. In Jesus, God has become both provider and provision, both the preparer of the feast and the feast itself, both the giver and the gift. Not empty calories; more than just taste. The love of God that is Jesus the Bread of life is real food for our hungry souls and spirits, real drink that is the very life of God flowing through us.

In inviting us "to feed on my flesh and drink of my blood," Jesus invites us to embrace the life of his Father: the life that finds joy in humble servanthood to others; the life that is centered in unconditional, total, sacrificial love; the life that seeks fulfillment not in the standards of this world but in the treasures of the next. In the "bread" he gives us to eat, Jesus shows us how to distinguish the values of God from the values of the marketplace; he instructs us on how to respond to the pressures and challenges of the world with justice and selflessness; he teaches us how to overcome our fears and doubts to become the people of compassion, reconciliation and hope that God created us to be.

*W*ith gratitude and humility,
we come to your table, O Lord,
to be nourished by the bread and wine
    of your Eucharist.
May we become what we receive here:
the bread that makes us one body in you,
the wine of your blood giving life
    to your justice and compassion,
the sacrament of your love in our midst.

Sunday 21 / Proper 16

Simon Peter answered Jesus, "Master, to whom shall we go?
You have the words of eternal life."

John 6: 60–69

"To dream the impossible ... "

In the musical *Man of La Mancha,* there is a moving scene
shortly after Don Quixote sings the show-stopping anthem "The
Impossible Dream." Miguel Cervantes, jailed during the Spanish
Inquisition, has been whiling away the time of his incarceration by
telling tales of his most famous creation, Don Quixote, the poor
deluded old man who imagines himself doing battle against man's
inhumanity to man.

Finishing the story, Cervantes is summoned to face his ac-
cusers. They ask him why poets and writers like himself are so
fascinated with madmen.

"I have seen life as it is," Cervantes explains. "Pain, misery,
hunger ... cruelty beyond belief. I have heard the singing from
taverns and the moans from bundles of filth on the streets. I have
been a soldier and seen my comrades fall in battle ... or die more
slowly under the lash in Africa. I have held them in my arms at
the final moment. These were men who saw life as it is, yet they
died despairing. No glory, no gallant last words ... only their eyes
filled with confusion, whimpering the question: *Why?* I do not
think they asked why they were dying, but why they had lived.
When life itself seems lunatic, who knows where madness lies?
Perhaps to be too practical is madness. To surrender dreams —
this may be madness. To seek treasure where there is only trash.
Too much sanity may be madness. And maddest of all, to see life
as it is and not as it should be."

Cervantes' words are not those of a madman but of every
thoughtful, perceptive human being who dares to wonder why

we become so concerned about not dying that we fail to live; why we become so obsessed with avoiding disaster that we refuse to experience the wonderful possibilities of life; why we become so afraid of being hurt or disillusioned that we refuse to risk love or commitment.

Today's concluding section of the "bread of life" discourse from John's Gospel is a turning point for the disciples of Jesus. Will they join the ranks of the skeptics, who have dismissed Jesus and his talk of "eating his flesh" or commit themselves to Jesus — and the shadows of the cross that are beginning to fall? We can hear the pain in Jesus' question: "Do you want to leave me, too?" Peter's simple, plaintive answer is the confession of faith voiced by disciples of every age who have come to sense the Spirit of God acting in and re-creating their lives.

Hopelessness can easily become a way of life; the sense that God has abandoned us or that God just doesn't exist in our lives can cripple us emotionally and spiritually. But the faithful disciple understands the reality that God is the only constant source of anything and everything that is good. The true demands of the Gospel are hard to "endure": the justice and reconciliation required of the faithful disciple runs counter to the conventions of society; the attitude of humble servanthood Jesus asks of us puts us at odds with the "me first/win at all costs" philosophy of our culture. The disciples who cannot "endure" Jesus' talk about giving his "flesh to eat" leave him and return to their "sane" but directionless, hopeless lives; But, as Peter acknowledges, the words of Jesus are the only way to transform and restore our lives and our world in the life of God.

The faith that Christ comes to reveal is not a warm fluffy blanket under which we hide from whatever we find unsettling or painful nor a protective coating designed to ward off every form of sin and evil. Faith is a light that illuminates our journey through life's challenges and obstacles, a lens through which we are able to see God's grace at work even in the most confusing and difficult times.

*I*n the noisy busy-ness of our lives, O Lord,
speak your word of peace and mercy.
In the anger and hatred marring our cities,
plant your compassion and justice in our midst.
In the darkness where we lose our way,
light your lamp of wisdom and grace
that we may find our way to your dwelling place.

Sunday 22 / Proper 17

"Nothing that enters from outside can defile a person; but the things that come out from within are what defile."

Mark 7: 1–8, 14–15, 21–23

On the street where you live ...

*T*wo houses stand across from each other on the same neighborhood street.

The first house is a chateau right out of the pages of *Home Beautiful.* It is beautifully designed and detailed. The yard is professionally landscaped; the manicured lawn would be the envy of any golf course. Elegant brocade and silk border the windows; the rooms are filled with fine furniture and antiques. Expensive late-model automobiles are parked in the driveway. A domestic staff keeps everything immaculate — from the wine cellar in the basement to the master suite upstairs.

The second house is far from being a dump but hardly the stuff of decorator magazines. Bicycles, ball games and small swimming pools have pot-marked the lawn. The driveway is strewn with skates, toys and sports equipment of all kinds. A durable van and sensible car, both with lots of miles and dents, are parked in the driveway. The house is decorated in a style that can most charitably be described as "eclectic" — large, stuffed sofas and chairs in the family room, bunk beds in the boys' rooms, a small desk in the girl's room that belonged to Mom when she was a girl. Keeping everything clean and neat is a challenge.

In the first house, it is always quiet. Although members of one family, the mother and father and children who live there are like ships passing in the night. Aside from the elegant parties for clients, the dining room table is never used. The father is away on business; the mother involved in a number of activities and projects; son and daughter have their own schedules, friends and activities. Four separate lives exist in the first house.

But there is always something going on in the second house. School work, games, a video, projects of all kinds light up every room. The menu is pretty simple and fast, but everyone pitches in to help — and everyone is at his or her place every night at the well-worn dinner table.

While cold formality chills the interior of the first house, love, compassion, forgiveness and support transform the second house into a real home.

Scott Russell Sanders writes: "Real estate ads offer houses for sale, not homes. A house is a garment easily put off or on, casually bought or sold; a home is skin. Merely change houses and you will be disoriented; change home and you bleed. When the shell you live in has taken on the savor of your love ... then your house is a home."[10]

In today's Gospel, Jesus challenges us to see beyond externals and facades to "inside" our souls and hearts to the place where God dwells: where love is born, where compassion reigns, where peace lives.

Today's Gospel recounts a controversy that Mark's first Christian readers understood all too well. A contentious debate raged in the early Church as to whether or not Christians should continue to observe the practices of Judaism. Mark recalls a similar debate that took place within the Judaism of Jesus' time when Jesus challenged the scribes' insistence that faithfulness to ceremonial washings and other rituals constitutes complete faithfulness to the will of God. In Mark's Gospel, Jesus scandalizes his hearers by proclaiming "nothing that enters a man from outside can make him impure; that which comes out of him, and only that, constitutes impurity." It is the good that one does, motivated by the spirit of the heart, that is important in the eyes of God, not how scrupulously one keeps the laws and rituals mandated by tradition.

Through the centuries of Judaism, the scribes had constructed a rigid maze of definitions, admonitions, principles and laws to explain the Pentateuch (summarized in Moses' eloquent words to the nation of Israel in today's first reading). As a result, the ethics of religion were often buried under a mountain of rules and taboos. Jesus' teachings re-focus the canons of Israel on the original covenant based on the wisdom and discernment of the human heart. Such a challenge widens the growing gulf between Jesus and the Jewish establishment.

Faith begins with encountering God in our hearts; our faith is expressed in the good that we do and the praise we offer in the depths of our hearts, not simply in words and rituals performed "outside" of ourselves. The kind of human beings we are begins in the values of the heart, the place where God dwells within — but the evil we are capable of, the hurt we inflict on others, the degrading of the world that God created also begins "within," when God is displaced by selfishness, greed, anger, or hatred.

The faithful disciple understands that it is the values of the heart, the compassion that dwells within, that makes even the messiest of houses holy places where the love of God dwells.

May your love and compassion
illuminate our hearts and spirits,
O God of graciousness,
transforming our rooms and houses
into loving homes of welcome and forgiveness.
Come, make your dwelling in our midst,
Making our tables and abodes
sacred spaces where your loving presence
loves, heals and protects.

They brought to him a deaf man who had a speech impediment and begged him to lay his hand on him. He took him off by himself away from the crowd. Jesus put his finger into the man's ears and, spitting, touched his tongue; he then looked up to heaven and groaned, and said to him, "Ephphatha!" — that is, "Be opened!"

Mark 7: 31–37
[Roman Lectionary]
Mark 7: 24–37
[Common Lectionary]

Life in its messiest

You're walking down a busy street and see him: the ubiquitous derelict looking for the handout, reeking of booze and filth, ranting and raving at everyone and no one. This would be a good time to cross the street.

She's not a bad kid, but for some reason she's been condemned to the outside, to the purgatory of the uncool and the unpopular. Never be cruel: A quick "Hi" when you see her in the hall, and keep moving.

So many issues we don't understand; so many problems other people struggle with that we keep at arms' length from our own lives. We hesitate to condemn, but we cling to easy slogans and beliefs that reduce the complexities of life to bumper stickers and sound bites. We'll happily write a check to help — just keep the problem away from me and my family.

While we avoid, walk around, nod politely and put off, Jesus welcomes, embraces and takes on life in its messiest and most unpleasant.

Note the details the evangelist Mark includes in today's Gospel: Encountering the deaf man, Jesus stops, makes time for him, and takes him away from the crowd to a quiet, safe place. Jesus then "put his finger into the man's ears and, spitting, touched his tongue." *Ick.* But Jesus doesn't just cure the deaf man with a fleeting word — by his touch, Jesus enters into the grit and grime, the struggle and pain of the man's struggle and, in doing so, brings hope and healing into his life. The Aramaic phrase *ephphatha* literally means "be released" — Jesus "releases" the man not only from his disability but from his isolation from the community and his alienation from God.

Jesus' curing of the deaf man with spittle (which, in Jesus' time, was considered curative) is an act of re-creation. Throughout Mark's Gospel, Jesus insists that his healings be kept quiet in order that his full identity be revealed and understood only in the light of his cross and resurrection. Isaiah's vision of a Messiah who would come with hope and healing (today's first reading) is realized in this episode from Mark's Gospel: the deaf hear, the silent are given voice, the lame "leap like a stag."

The exhortation *Ephphatha!* is not only addressed to the man born deaf but to his disciples both then and now who fail to hear and see and speak the presence of God in their very midst. We, too, can bring healing and life to those who need the support, the affirmation, the sense of loving and being loved that the simple act of listening can give.

In times of grief, despair and failure, we can be "deaf" to the presence of God in the love and compassion of others; or we can become so preoccupied with the noise and clamor of the marketplace that we are unable to hear the voices of those we love and who love us. *Ephphatha* is Jesus' healing of our hearts and spirits, the healing of our own "deafness" to the cries of our brothers and sisters in need.

The Gospel pericope in the Common lectionary for this Sunday begins with another healing story (Mark 7: 24–30). Despite his requests for secrecy, Jesus' reputation as a worker of wonders is spreading. He seeks refuge from the demands of the crowds in a small house in Tyre. A Syrophnoenician woman intrudes on Jesus' privacy, pleading with him to cure her daughter "possessed" by a "demon" — the catch-all diagnosis for any number of inexplicable illnesses. Being a woman and a non-Jew, she humbles herself at Jesus' feet. Jesus sounds uncharacteristically brusque in dismissing her (although Mark's readers would not be put off by Jesus' refusal to help this Gentile woman; Jews often expressed their scorn for Gentiles and pagans by referring to them as "dogs") — but this Gentile woman is driven by a mother's love and a trust in God's providence that is more than a match for Judaic contempt. Again, Jesus holds up the faith of an "unclean" Gentile as a model for "the children" of Israel to embrace and be embraced by God's Spirit of compassion. In Jesus, the barriers among peoples are broken down; the reign of God he comes to proclaim welcomes every human being, all children of God.

*L*ord, may *ephphatha* be our prayer:
Release us from our fears,
our pride, our self-centeredness
that makes us deaf to you.
Open our hearts to the cries
of our brothers and sisters in need
and make our hands the means
of healing and hope for all.

Along the way Jesus asked his disciples, "Who do you say I am?" Peter said to him in reply, "You are the Christ ... "
Jesus began to teach them that the Son of Man must suffer greatly and be rejected by the elders, the chief priests, and the scribes and be killed, and rise after three days. He spoke this openly. Then Peter took him aside and began to rebuke him. At this he turned around and, looking at his disciples, rebuked Peter and said, "Get behind me, Satan. You are thinking not as God does, but as human beings do."

Mark 8: 27–35

Bringing Christ to my daughter's attackers

A husband and wife are involved in the detention ministry at a prison near their home, assisting at Communion services one Saturday a month. The couple have been both surprised and humbled by the faith and sense of the sacred they have seen among the incarcerated.

But then one Saturday night their oldest daughter was mugged. She was talking to two friends in a restaurant parking lot when two young men approached her for a light. As she dug out her lighter, there was suddenly a gun at her head. The two men grabbed the girls' purses and were gone. It was as quick as that: the hit-and-run loss of her wallet and the death of her innocence.

Mom and Dad were grateful that their daughter wasn't hurt — but their attitude toward their volunteer work at the prison started to change. So far they had been able to separate the men from their pasts — but how could they look at these inmates the same way? They were afraid that they would look at each man and wonder, *Did you hold a gun to someone's daughter's head? Did you threaten to kill her? Did you steal not just her wallet, but her faith in the goodness of humanity?*

Could they continue their work at the prison? Could they put aside their hurt and anger at what happened to their daughter? After much soul-searching, the couple has decided to continue. They have come to a new understanding about what Christ has called them to do in their work at the prison.

The mother, Valerie Schultz, writes in *America* Magazine:

"So much has been given to me: life, love, children, health, wealth, freedom, privilege. I return so few of my gifts to God: in fact, I hoard them. My involvement in prison ministry requires an embarrassingly small amount of time and effort and presence. Any good I may do is equally small ...

"I believe that we have been called to visit the imprisoned; I believe I hear that call clearly. And it is not complicated, unless I make it that way. Jesus did not say, 'When I was in prison, you made excuses for me, you condoned my crimes, you sprang me by smuggling in a fake ID.' What he said was, 'I was in prison, and you visited me.'

"To visit: that's all he's asking. But by treating inmates like fellow human beings, by focusing on rehabilitation and amends, by bringing Christ to the hearts and lips of those who are so often unloved and unreachable, who lack the freedom and privilege I take for granted, perhaps future crimes will be averted and future victims spared. Perhaps minds and behaviors can be changed. Perhaps someone else's daughter will go home unaccosted, and in that way I continue to visit the imprisoned, and still look my own daughter in the eye."[11]

The question Jesus poses to his disciples he poses to us and to every disciple of every age: *Who do you say I am?* Every decision we make, every action we take, proclaims who we believe this Jesus is and what his Gospel means to us. Sometimes our answering that question demands that we put aside our own fears, hurts and self-importance to say to ourselves and our community, *You are the Christ — You are the Christ God has sent to teach us his way of humble gratitude, joyful service, and just peace.*

While we eagerly seek to follow Christ the worker of wonders, the consoling and compassionate Good Shepherd, we don't even want to hear about the condemned Christ struggling under the weight of the cross on the road to Calvary. In today's Gospel, Peter mirrors our own guarded, qualified response to the call to discipleship.

Caesar Philippi was a bazaar of worship places and temples, with altars erected to every concept of the divinity from the gods of Greece to the godhead of Caesar. Amid this marketplace of gods, Jesus asks Peter and the Twelve, "Who do people say that I am? ... Who do *you* say that I am?" This is a turning point in Mark's Gospel: Until now, Mark's Jesus has been reluctant to have people believe in him only because of his miracles. For the first time in Mark's Gospel, Jesus talks about dark things ahead: rejection, suffering, death and resurrection (concepts that the disciples are unable to grasp).

In this incident (recorded by all three Synoptics), Peter immediately confesses his faith in Jesus as the Messiah — the Messiah of victory and salvation. But when Jesus begins to speak of a Messiah who will suffer rejection and death, Peter objects. Peter's reaction mirrors our own: We prefer to follow the popular, happy Jesus, the healing and comforting Jesus — but we back away from the suffering, humble, unsettling Jesus of the cross.

We cannot belong to the company of Jesus unless we embrace the Crucified One's spirit of generous servanthood. Taking up our crosses — however heavy the wood, whatever steep Calvary we must climb — sometimes demands a difficult change in our perspectives and attitudes. Only in "denying ourselves" in order to imitate the humble selflessness of Christ do we experience the true depth of our faith; only in embracing his compassion and humility in our lives do we enable the Spirit of God to renew and transform our world in God's life and love.

May your spirit of compassion and humility
enable us to walk with you, Lord Jesus,
not only in the morning of Easter peace
but in the darkness of Good Friday suffering.
May we struggle with our own crosses

in the certain hope
that your shoulder bears its weight with us,
that your hand leads us through every suffering,
that your light illuminates the way we make our way
from confusion to wisdom,
from doubt to faith,
from suffering to wholeness,
from death to life.

Sunday 25 / Proper 20

They had been discussing among themselves on the way who was the greatest. Then Jesus sat down and called the Twelve, and said to them, "If anyone wishes to be first, he shall be last of all and the servant of all." He placed a child in their midst, and putting his arms around the child, he said to them, "Whoever receives one child such as this in my name, receives me; and whoever receives me, receives not me but the One who sent me."

Mark 9: 30–37

All you can eat

*M*om — or Dad — is feeding the baby. The child is sitting up in the high chair, wearing a bib that will do little to prevent food from finding its way into the baby's clothes and face and hair; the child has no interest in food, having discovered that the chair's plastic tray makes a great drum.

Mom has prepared a small dish of pureed vegetables for the baby's lunch. She loads a baby-size spoon with the greenish goop and pilots the spoon towards the child's mouth.

What happens next? If you've ever fed a baby, you know.

First, Mom instinctively opens her own mouth wide. Only then will the baby follow suit. That's because it's impossible to spoon-feed a baby without opening your own mouth wide as you bring the food in for a landing.

Try it sometime.

Feeding a child is a great image for appreciating Jesus' point in today's Gospel. Catherine O'Connell-Cahill writes that, as parents hand on their faith to their children, "we find that our own spiritual hunger is being fed, too. The experience can bring us back to church or prompt us to update what we know and believe, as we grow from the faith of childhood to a more appropriate version."[12]

Christ calls us to embrace the simple but profound faith that we seek to teach our children: to love God and one another with honesty and faithfulness, without condition or expectation, putting aside every "adult" rationalization and agenda. Only in "opening" our own hearts to Jesus' Gospel of uncomplicated and straightforward kindness, compassion, generosity and forgiveness, can we help our sons and daughters become authentic followers of the Jesus of selflessness and compassion.

Different hopes and expectations — and agendas — collide in today's Gospel. A somber Jesus speaks cryptically of the death and resurrection awaiting him in Jerusalem, while those closest to him argue about their own greatness and status in the Messiah's reign (that must have been quite a conversation to elicit such a strong reaction from Jesus). The disciples, long resigned to their people's humiliation and subjugation, dream of a kingdom of power and influence in which ambition is exalted; Jesus explains to them (yet again) that the Messiah's reign will be a kingdom of spirit and conversion in which humble service to others is exalted.

Jesus outlines here the great paradox of discipleship: *Do you wish to be first? Then become last. Do you seek to attain greatness? Then become small. Do you want to be masters? Then humble yourselves to become the servants of those you wish to rule.*

To emphasize the point, Jesus picks up a little child and places the child in the midst of these would-be rulers and influence peddlers. A child has no power in the affairs of society nor offers anything to adults in terms of career advancement or prestige enhancement; just the opposite is true: a child needs everything. To be "great" in the reign of God, Jesus says, one must become the "servant" of the "child," the poor, the needy, the lost.

In their simple joy and wonder of the world they are constantly discovering, in their ready acceptance of our love, in their total dependence on us for their nurturing and growth, children are the ideal teachers of the Spirit of humble servanthood and constant thanksgiving that Jesus asks of those who would be his followers. "Child-like faith" is never dissuaded or discouraged, never becomes cynical or jaded, never ceases to be amazed and grateful for the many ways God reveals his presence in our lives. The power of such "simple faith" is its ability to overcome every rationalization, fear, complication and agenda in order to mirror the selflessness of Christ Jesus.

The poorest and neediest, the forgotten and rejected, the "least" and the "lowly," represented by the child in today's Gospel, are signs of God's grace in our midst. Christ calls us to embrace the uncomplicated but genuine faith of the child, faith that we adults sadly "outgrow": faith that is centered in loving God and others without condition or expectation. In the service we give and respect we afford to all as sons and daughters of God, Jesus says, we welcome into our midst the very presence of God. Our love for them mirrors the love of God for us despite our failings, our sins, our distortion of God's creation for our own self-centered ends. Only in putting ourselves in the humble service of the lowly child can we hope to claim a place in the kingdom of God.

*C*hrist Jesus,
may we find our life's "greatness"
in imitating your own example
   of humble, generous servanthood.
Open our eyes to recognize you in one another;
open our arms to welcome the child in our midst –
the poor, the forgotten, the ignored, the marginalized;
open our hearts to create God's reign
   of compassion and peace
in our time and place.

"Anyone who gives you a cup of water to drink because you belong to Christ, amen, I say to you, will surely not lose his reward. "Whoever causes one of these little ones who believes in me to sin, it would be better for him if a great millstone were put around his neck and he were thrown into the sea."

Mark 9: 38–43, 45, 47–48

Millstones

A couple had just completed their annual tax return. It had been a good year: their portfolio had performed well, they sold property at a premium, and they both earned substantial raises at work. But as they reviewed the records, they were stunned at the paltry sum they had given charity; they were embarrassed at how little meaningful support they had given to groups and organizations that were doing important work in their own town.

For if your wealth should keep you from giving to the poor, sell your stocks and bonds and liquidate your assets; better you should enter heaven without a penny to your name than be condemned to hell with a well-performing portfolio.

The guys had heard rumblings about some changes at the work site. Then one morning they met their new foreman — an MIT-educated engineer named Santos. Santos had three things going against him — he was young, he was educated, and he was — well, "new." The guys took an *O.K., kid, prove yourself* attitude — and Santos delivered. Santos knew what he was doing — and he easily got every worker on board. The guys came to admire Santos' skill and work ethic and respected Santos as Santos respected them.

And if your prejudices lead you to reject or underestimate someone because of their age or gender or religion or heritage,

*cut off your self-righteousness. Better for you to enter into the king-
dom of God with all your brothers and sisters than be thrown into
Gehenna with your pride.*

The numbers just didn't add up. He had gone over the figures
again and again. He went to see the president, who expressed his
concern and promised to look into it. But nothing happened. In
the meantime, the company started hemorrhaging money. Finally,
he went to the F.E.C. His blowing the whistle on the fraud cost
him his job. But, while he and his family struggled through a long
drought of unemployment, he could look his children in the eye.
He had done the right thing.

*And if job security leads you to compromise your ethics and
integrity, better for you to enter into life unemployed than be
thrown into Gehenna with a good salary-and-benefits package.*

In his rather harsh words about "cutting off" and "plucking
out," Jesus calls us to realize that discipleship means letting nothing — *nothing* — dissuade us or derail us in our search for the
things of God, not allowing the pursuit of wealth, security, or
status detach us from the things of God or diminish the love of
God we cherish in family and friends.

Jesus' admonition is the result of the apostle John's troubling
report that someone was spotted cashing in on Jesus' growing
reputation as a healer by invoking Jesus' name to cast out a demon.
The people of Jesus' time believed that any unexplainable illness or
physical infirmity was caused by some "demon" and that "demon"
could be exorcised by invoking the name of a still more powerful
spirit. John's concern, at first reading, appears to have some merit
— but recall the on-going battle among the disciples as to who is
the greatest among them. Jesus responds, therefore, by condemning his disciples' jealousy and intolerance, warning against an elit-
ist view of faith that diminishes the good done by those we consider
"outsiders." Whoever acts out of compassion and generosity, who
is motivated out of mercy and justice, is part of Jesus' company.

Today's Gospel selection includes Jesus' exhortation that it is
better lose one's limb if it leads one to sin. Two notes about these
final verses:

The "millstone" Jesus speaks of was the large piece of stone that was turned by a pack animal to grind grain. Drowning a criminal by tying him to one of these large heavy stones was a method of execution in Rome and Palestine.

Gehenna was a vile place in Jewish history. The young King Ahaz (2 Chronicles 38: 3) practiced child immolation to the "fire god" at Gehenna. In Jesus' time, Gehenna, a ravine outside Jerusalem, served as the city's refuse site. Gehenna became synonymous with our concept of hell for the Jews.

We may not think of ourselves as perfect, but we do (however unconsciously) consider our perspective of the world and our own belief and value systems to be the standards that others would be wise to embrace. To "act in Jesus' name" demands "letting go" of our own ego, interests and control in order to imitate the selfless servanthood of the Gospel Jesus. The struggle to follow Jesus is "detach" ourselves from the "sinful" so we can "attach" ourselves to the things of God.

*M*ay our humble and imperfect attempts, O Lord,
to imitate your compassion and justice
make us worthy to be part of your company.
Open our eyes to see you in others;
open our hands that we may give to others
    from our need;
guide our steps that we may let nothing
distract us or dissuade us
on our journey to the Father's dwelling place.

"Because of the hardness of your hearts [Moses] wrote this commandment ... "
" 'They are no longer two but one flesh.' Therefore, what God has joined together, no human being must separate ...
"Whoever does not accept the kingdom of God like a child will not enter it."

Mark 10: 2–16

Whites and darks, bless the Lord!

*T*he night before their 10th anniversary, they did what they had done just about every Thursday night since they were married: the laundry.

In the family room, with the baseball game on, they sorted the mountain of just-laundered clothes. She smoothed their daughter's tees; he folded their son's Spiderman pajamas.

She matched up what seemed like hundreds of socks; he separated the various undershirts and underpants.

As he kept one eye on the ball game while they worked, it struck her how their laundry had grown over the years. She remembered that first year of their marriage when they would hurry off to that dingy Laundromat near their one-bedroom apartment with their single basket of clothes. They were both working and in school; time — and money — were tight. Now they had this beautiful home with (thank God!) a washing machine and dryer.

With the birth of their children, the single basket quadrupled, with diapers, play clothes and school clothes, and towels. There were, of course, disasters along the way: the time he shrunk her beautiful cashmere sweater; the time little Bobby left crayons in his pocket, turning all the whites into a bizarre shade of reddish orange.

As she fluffed and folded the week's laundry, she was overcome with a sense of gratitude. While the laundry was not their favorite household chore, tonight she saw these shirts and socks and shorts and uniforms as cotton and polyblend signs of God's goodness.

Just then, her daydream was snapped. As she reached into the basket to grab a towel, he grabbed the same towel. She looked up and smiled; he smiled back, not knowing what that tear in her eye was all about. His touch still sent a shiver up and down her spine. Yep, the marriage is still working, she thought.

Tomorrow night they would go out to dinner to celebrate 20 years of doing laundry together.

A couple's life together — a life centered in trust, forgiveness and love — and their generous response to the vocation of parenthood model the unfathomable and profound love of God, love that lets go rather than clings, love that happily gives rather than takes, love that liberates rather than imprisons. The sacrament of marriage, as Jesus taught, is a total giving and sharing by each spouse so that the line between "his" and "hers" disappears into only "us."

In today's Gospel, Jesus cites the Genesis account of the creation of man and woman (today's first reading) to emphasize that husband and wife are equal partners in the covenant of marriage ("the two become one body"). The language of Genesis reflects the Creator intention that the marriage union possess the same special covenantal nature as God's covenant with Israel. Jesus again appeals to the spirit of the Law rather than arguing legalities: It is the nature of their marriage covenant that husband and wife owe to one another total and complete love and mutual respect in sharing responsibility for making their marriage succeed.

The question of divorce was among the most divisive issues in Jewish society. The Book of Deuteronomy (24: 1) stipulated that a husband could divorce his wife for "some indecency." Interpretations of exactly what constituted "indecency" varied greatly, ranging from adultery to accidentally burning the evening meal. Further, the wife was regarded under the Law as a husband's chattel, having neither legal right to protection nor recourse to seeking a divorce on her own. In Biblical times, there was little appreciation of love and commitment in marriage — marriages were always arranged in the husband's favor, the husband could divorce his wife for just about any reason, the woman was treated little better than property. Divorce, then, was tragically common among the Jews of Jesus' time.

But, seen through the prism of the Gospel, marriage is more than a "contract" between two "parties" but a *sacrament* — a living sign of God's presence and grace in our midst, the manifestation of the love of God, a love that knows neither condition nor limit in its ability to give and forgive. Jesus appeals to his followers to embrace the Spirit of love that is the basis of God's "law" — that we are called to act out a sense of the compassion and justice of God rather than fulfilling legalisms and detached rituals.

Today's Gospel reading also includes Mark's story of Jesus' welcoming the children who come to see him. Again, Jesus holds up the model of a child's simplicity and humility as the model for the servant-disciple. A child's marvelous sense of wonder, inquisitiveness and simplicity that deflates adult "logic" and the "conventional wisdom" and make us look at the essence of our actions and our beliefs model for us how to respond in faith to Jesus' call to discipleship.

*C*hrist of compassion,
be the ever-present, unseen Wedding Guest
    in our homes,
transforming every moment and milestone,
every joy and discovery,
every struggle and mundane chore
into manifestations of your love.
May our lives as spouses and families
be living sacraments of your love
for all your children.

Sunday 28 / Proper 23

Jesus, looking at the rich young man, loved him and said to him, "You are lacking in one thing. Go, sell what you have, and give to the poor, and you will have treasure in heaven; then come, follow me." At that statement, his face fell, and he went away sad, for he had many possessions.

Mark 10: 17–30

And how do I make out the check?

One Sunday morning, the parish's religious education director was making the fall appeal for volunteer teachers for the new school year. Many young parents listened politely to her request for adults to share their faith with the children of the parish, of the call each one of us receives in baptism to be ministers of the Word, of the great gift each one of us possesses to share how God is present in our own lives. At the end of Mass, many congratulated the religious education director on her presentation. "What you said was so important. We want good teachers for our children. But, given our schedules, we couldn't possibly teach. But could we write a check to help in your work?"

Every year charities host golf tournaments, dinners and benefits on behalf of all kinds of worthy causes in medicine, education and the arts. Wanting to be perceived as "good neighbors" and "socially responsible" — especially when compared to their competitors — companies will write sizable checks (all tax deductible, of course) for the cause. But it's more business and public relations than compassion; the designated charity is a line item on the tax form, not a human being whose life has been touched and changed.

We fear for our children. We want to protect them from the scourge of drugs, alcohol, sex and violence. We want them to grow up to become compassionate and loving men and women, with a deeply-held sense of morality and ethics. And we will happily write a check to any institution, organization or sports league that promises to do that for our children. But it often escapes us that the more profitable investment would be in spending more time with our kids, strengthening that bond of trust and love that is the ultimate grace in coping with life's twists and turns.

In his encounter with the young man, Jesus demands of him what he is not prepared to give. Jesus asks him not just to help the poor but to *become* poor, to find the treasure of heaven by giving up the treasure of earth

The young rich man in today's Gospel is one of the most pitiable characters in the Jesus story. Clearly, Jesus' teachings and healings have touched something in him but his enthusiasm outdistances his commitment. Assuring Jesus that he has kept the "you shall NOTS" of the Law, Jesus confronts the rich young man with the "you SHALLS" of the reign of God: "Go and sell what you have and give it to the poor."

And, as Mark describes it, the man's face fell as "he went away sad." He can't bring himself to do it. His faith is not strong enough to give up the treasure he possesses for the "treasure in heaven." The young man walks away, disappointed certainly, and perhaps feeling even somewhat disillusioned that his hero Jesus is not what he thought and hoped he would be.

Then Jesus, speaking to his disciples, turns another Jewish belief upside down. Popular Jewish morality was simple: prosperity was a sign that one had found favor with God. There was a definite "respectability" to being perceived as wealthy and rich (how little have things changed!). Great wealth, Jesus points out, is actually a hindrance to heaven: Rich people tend to look at things in terms of price, of value, of the "bottom line." Jesus preaches *detachment* from things in order to become completely *attached* to the life and love of God.

Throughout the Gospel, Jesus points to the inadequacy of viewing religion as a series of codes and laws. The young man was no different than his contemporaries in seeing one's relationship with God as based on a series of negatives ("you shall not"). Discipleship is not based on NOT doing and avoiding but on DOING and acting in the love of God. Jesus calls us not to follow a code of conduct but, rather, to embrace the Spirit that gives meaning and purpose to the great commandment. Jesus asks everything of us as the cost of being his disciple — but Jesus asks only what we have, not what we don't have. Each one of us possesses talents and resources, skills and assets that we have been given by God for the work of making the kingdom of God a reality in the here and now.

*G*od of every good thing,
unclench our hands that we may let go
of the things we grasp;
pull us out of the spiral
of being consumed by what we consume.
May we realize that everything you have given us
is entrusted to us
to build your kingdom of justice and peace.
May we not just help the poor
but become poor in spirit and humility;
may we not just console the suffering
but suffer with them;
may we not avoid sin
but take on the work of changing those situations
in which fear and evil crush and destroy.

Sunday 29 / Proper 24

"You know that those who are recognized as rulers over the Gentiles lord it over them and their great ones make their authority felt. But it shall not be so among you. Rather, whoever wishes to be first among you will be the slave of all."

Mark 10: 35–45

Memories are made of this ...

*T*he founding pastor of a congregation was invited back to the church for the 25th anniversary of the parish. Former members of the church traveled hundreds of miles to be part of the celebration.

One by one, folks came up to the priest:

You married us and baptized our children.

Do you remember that sermon you preached on forgiveness? It moved me enough to call my brother and end our stupid feud.

When we moved here, I had never moved in my entire life. You and the parish did so much to make this place our home.

The priest began to do some of his own reminiscing.

Do you remember the program we did "Celebrating Lent"?

Remember the different pot-luck theme nights?

What about our "Living Waters Plan" to get everyone in the parish involved? That was one of the most successful programs we did.

But the priest's reminiscences were met with blank looks. He continued his litany of "brilliant ideas" which had consumed his time and energy as pastor. But while the programs had been a source of great pride for him, they were not part of the collective memory of the congregation. They had their own litany:

Do you remember when you came to the hospital to baptize our baby?

When I was having a tough time, you gave me this copy of the
Serenity Prayer — look, I still have it.
You gave me this article. It helped me through my divorce.
The priest remembers of the evening:
    "That which made a difference in the lives of the people I
served was not my brilliant program ideas, strategic plans or my
efforts to impress them with my leadership/management skills ...
What they remembered was not my brilliance, but those moments
when I got out of the way and God touched them."[13]

Christ's call to be the servant of others means to let God work
through our own efforts to love, to forgive, to secure justice, to
support and help. Seeking such "greatness" means never to be
discouraged by the seeming smallness or insignificance of what
we are able to do for others. A disciple's faith enables one to experience joy, not in the acclaim we receive for what we do or in
the success we can measure or list on a resume, but in the joy we
bring into the lives of others one small act at a time, in the small
stones we can place together one at a time to build the kingdom
of God in our own time and place.

In the Gospel reading four Sundays ago (just a chapter ago in
Mark's Gospel), Jesus admonished his disciples for their pointless
argument among themselves as to who was the most important.
James and John apparently did not get the message.

In today's Gospel account, the two sons of Zebedee — who,
with Peter, make up Jesus' inner circle — ask for the places of
honor and influence when Jesus begins his reign. James and John
proclaim their willingness to "drink the cup" of suffering and
share in the "bath" or "baptism" of pain Jesus will experience
(the Greek word used is *baptizein,* meaning to immerse oneself in
an event or situation). Jesus finally tells them that the assigning of
such honors is the prerogative of God the Father.

Most readers share the other disciples' indignation at the
incredible nerve of James and John to make such a request (Matthew, in his Gospel, casts the two brothers in a little better light by
having their mother make the request — Matthew 20: 20.) Jesus
calls the disciples together to try again to make them understand
that he calls them to greatness through service. Jesus' admonition

to them is almost a pleading: *If you really understand me and what I am about, if you want to be my disciple, if you truly seek to be worthy of my name, then you must see the world differently and respond to its challenges with a very different set of values. The world may try to justify vengeance rather than forgiveness, to glorify self-preservation over selflessness, to insist on preserving the system and convention for the sake of compassion and justice* — but it cannot be that way with you.

Jesus' admonition — "It shall not be so among you" — is perhaps the greatest challenge of the Gospel, calling us not to accept "business as usual," not to accept injustice and estrangement as "the way things are," not to justify our flexible morals and ethics with the mantra "everybody does it."

To be an authentic disciple of Jesus means to put ourselves in the humble, demanding role of servant to others, to intentionally seek the happiness and fulfillment of those we love regardless of the cost to ourselves. Sometimes, like the pastor discovers, it means putting aside our own grand plans and need for control to take on the less glamorous but no less important role of empathetic listener and supportive friend.

*C*hrist of compassion,
may we, who have been baptized
    into your death and resurrection,
be immersed in your Spirit of humility
    and servanthood.
Help us to see you in one another;
to discover the blessings of generosity;
to seek greatness in service to all
and as ministers of your mercy.

Sunday 30 / Proper 25

Bartimaeus, a blind man, the son of Timaeus, sat by the road-side begging. "Jesus, Son of David, have mercy on me!"
"Master, I want to see."
Jesus said to him, "Go your way; your faith has saved you."

Mark 10: 46–52

Revelatory ants

*D*enise Roy, in her wonderful book, *My Monastery Is a Minivan: Where the Daily is Divine and the Routine Becomes Prayer,* tells of the night she spotted an ant crawling across her sheet as she and her husband were getting ready for bed. Then she saw another ant. And another. She followed the trail to a wall in a linen closet where a zillion ants were happily scaling their way down three shelves to their midnight snack: a forgotten bottle of cherry-flavored liquid Children's Tylenol. She and her husband sprayed Raid all over the wall, freezing the dead ants in place. They opened windows and turned on fans until the toxic smell dissipated. Finally, after ten thorough inspections of their bed, they crawled under the sheets. Because it was so late, they left the clean-up of the ants until morning — but as soon as the alarm went off, Mom and Dad were immediately caught up in the family's usual busy morning routine.

"What I'm about to report is not a little embarrassing," Denise Roy writes. "Not for just one day, not for just one week, not just for one month — but for more than three months, those ants stayed glued to my wall, I'm not sure exactly what happened. Mostly, I think I stopped seeing."

"Now this onset of blindness may have been aggravated by the fact that the walls themselves were not a pretty sight to begin with. When we bought the house five years ago, we hated the bedroom wallpaper and were going to take it down and paint the walls before moving in. But one thing led to another, and it just never got done."

Four years went by before she finally tackled the ugly wallpaper. But she discovered it was a bigger job than she had imagined: the wallpaper was glued really well and shredded and stuck as she tried to remove it. After a few hours, she stopped peeling for the day and planned to get back to it later. You know what happened. "Even the ants, when they went marching up our walls, had to weave in and out of the grooves in the wallpaper. Ultimately, I just grew blind to the whole mess," she writes.

The moment of revelation came one day while visiting her sister, "who has three young children, one lizard, two cats, and two rats. I went into the bedroom to get something and saw that her bed wasn't made, clothes strewn around, and a few toys were on the floor.

"How can she live like this? I thought.

"Grateful that I was not like her, I returned home and went upstairs. As I walked into my own bedroom, the ants started laughing at me."[14]

In the busy-ness of our lives, we become blind to the messes that begin to take over; in the many demands placed on us, we no longer see the possibilities for doing good and affirming things. We can re-cast a situation to justify or rationalize our own self-absorption, our lack of compassion, our avoiding anyone or anything unpleasant, our refusal to accept responsibility for our actions (or inactions). As he restores to Bartimaeus not only physical sight but a sense of the reality of God's love for him, Christ comes to restore our "sight" to see God's sacred presence in our lives, to heal us of our blindness to the sins of selfishness and hatred we too easily explain away. Our deepest prayer is the cry of the blind Bartimaeus: "Master, I want to see" — to "see" with the human heart, to perceive in the spirit, to comprehend in the wisdom of God.

Mark's story of the blind Bartimaeus, which takes place just before Jesus' Palm Sunday entry into Jerusalem, is as much a "call" story as a healing story. For Mark, Bartimaeus is model of faith. The blind beggar calls out to Jesus using the Messianic title "Son of David." He first asks, not for his sight, but for compassion: He understands that this Jesus operates out of a spirit of love and compassion for humanity and places his faith in that spirit. Ironically, the blind Bartimaeus "sees" in Jesus the spirit of compassionate service that, until now, his "seeing" disciples have been unable to comprehend.

As Bartimaeus realizes, Christ comes to heal our spiritual and moral blindness and open our eyes to recognize the Spirit of God in every person and to discern the way of God in all things; he opens our eyes as well as hearts and spirits to new images of a world made whole by the grace of God, of lives transformed by the love of God.

*C*ome, Lord, and restore our sight
that we may realize your sacred presence
    in our midst.
Heal us of our blindness to our selfishness
    and hatred
and illuminate our vision
that we may comprehend your grace and blessings
    in our lives.

Sunday 31 / Proper 26

> " 'You shall love the Lord your God with all your heart, and with all your soul, and with all your mind, and with all your strength ... ' 'You shall love your neighbor as yourself ...' There is no commandment greater than these."

Mark 12: 28–34

The gift of listening

A young psychiatrist, new to the profession, realized that she needed help in dealing with her own problems, so she made an appointment to meet with a psychiatrist herself. But fifteen minutes into the first session, she knew this doctor would not be able to help her — the doctor's questions were too simple, her expression emotionless; frankly, she didn't think this doctor was too bright.

While she wanted to discontinue the sessions, she was too busy with her own work to find another doctor, so she continued meeting with her. And all she would do, week after week, was cry. The doctor never said anything wise or wonderful. She would occasionally tug at her skirt or rotate her wedding rings, but said nothing nor gave any hint of understanding or compassion or wisdom. Every week, during their hour together, the young woman would cry and think about how to leave this psychiatrist who clearly did not understand her.

Eventually, the young resident felt better and decided to move on with her life and career.

That's when she learned something important about her profession. She writes:

"After we said good-bye, I realized something: All along, she had known how I felt about her. All those years, she had known I thought she was stupid. She had let me think it, because she understood — which I did not — that what I needed was not someone I could admire, not someone shamanistic, but someone who would listen to me while I cried ...

"I hope that one day I will be able to let my patients think I am stupid, while I am listening to them cry."[15]

A psychiatrist sacrifices her ego — how she is perceived by her colleague — in order to bring healing to her patient. Such complete and unconditional love and mercy extended to others mirrors the love and mercy of God; in acts of charity and selflessness we mirror in the very life of God. In the two-fold "great commandment" we discover a purpose to our lives much greater and larger than ourselves and our own needs, interests, prejudices and biases; in loving God in one another, we find the ultimate meaning of the gifts of faith and life.

In today's Gospel from Mark, Jesus "synthesizes" his Gospel in his fusing of the "great commandment." The Jews knew these two commandments well. To this day, observant Jews pray twice daily the *Shema*: to love God "with all your heart, and with all your soul and with all your strength." The word *shema* means "to hear," and comes from the first words of the prayer, "Hear, O Israel …" The text for the *Shema*, which is also inscribed in the *mezuzah*, the small container affixed to the door of every Jewish home, is found in Deuteronomy 6: 4–6 (today's first reading). While the Torah outlined a Jew's responsibility to one's neighbors, Jesus is the first to make of these two instructions a single commandment: "There is no other commandment greater than these." The only way we can adequately celebrate our love for God is in extending that love to our neighbors.

To love as God calls us to love demands every fiber of our being — heart, soul, mind, and strength. It is in our love and compassion for one another that humanity most closely resembles God; it is in our charity and selflessness that we participate in God's work of creation.

*F*ather, you are the Source and Center of our lives.
By the light of your Word,
may we realize our "connectedness" to you,
    and through you, to one another.
May we be embraced by your compassion
in the love we extend to one another;
may we be reconciled with you
in our forgiveness of one another;
may we be worthy to be your sons and daughters
by honoring every human being as our brother and sister.

Sunday 32 / Proper 27

"Beware of the scribes, who like to go around in long robes and accept greetings in the marketplaces, seats of honor in synagogues, and places of honor at banquets. They devour the houses of widows and, as a pretext recite lengthy prayers ...
" ... this poor widow put in more than all the other contributors to the treasury."

Mark 12: 38–44

The most for her money

*O*n her way to her weekly yoga class, a woman stopped at a gas station that had a coin-operated vacuum cleaner. The woman dropped in a couple of quarters and went to work, scrubbing the floor mats and carpets, praying she could suck up the hair, dried mud, and chocolate-chip scone crumbs in the allotted three minutes.

As she vacuumed, a man dressed in jeans and a T-shirt, with a black leather pouch, appeared.

"I'm sorry, ma'am, but do you have any spare change you could give me for a bus ticket?"

"No!" the woman shouted over the whirring vacuum. "This is not a good time!"

"I'm sorry," the man repeated and walked on.

The woman immediately regretted her rudeness. Finishing her vacuuming, she fished out a crumbled dollar bill from the glove department. The man had walked across the street and was sitting on a bus stop bench. She walked over and held out the dollar, "Do you still need bus fare?" Startled, the man said, "Why yes, ma'am. God bless you, ma'am."

The woman nodded curtly and went on to her yoga class, annoyed at having been called "ma'am" three times in five minutes.

As she went through her yoga exercises and chants, she thought about what had just happened. She had read newspaper articles in which so-called "homeless" people admitted that they collected 20 dollars an hour just sitting beside a stoplight holding a cardboard sign. She had heard tales of people pretending to need change for a phone call, a hamburger and, yes, bus fare. She had convinced herself that she had been duped by the stranger.

But as she sat on her $25 yoga mat at her $10-per session yoga class, having just vacuumed the remnants of chocolate-chip scones from her $25,000 car, she realized: "Who am I to deny someone a dollar for any reason? Who am I to refuse to give when I so obviously have a surplus? This man's bag may have been stuffed with crumpled dollar bills like the one I'd just handed him, but all that concerned me was that a man had humbled himself enough to ask for help from a stranger."

The woman, humbled herself, remembers: "I was proud of one thing that morning — I had paused to look into the man's eyes before I [went on]. They were dark and anxious, embarrassed, but grateful. Next time, no matter whether he appears as man, woman or child, I'll pause another moment to ask him where he is going. And then I will wish him a safe journey."[16]

In her encounter with the beggar, this woman comes to understand the sister values of humility and gratitude. Before God's goodness, our own sense of entitled honor fades; caught up in the love of God, our sense of self diminishes.

The widow's penny is the marriage of humility and gratitude. Preaching in the Jerusalem temple days before the Last Supper and his crucifixion, Jesus indicts the scribes for their lavish but empty show of faith. The scribes, in their haughty and arrogant attitude, are the antithesis of what Jesus wants his disciples to be. In Jesus' time, scribes, as the accepted experts of the Law, could serve as trustees of a widow's estate. As their fee, they took a portion of the estate. Obviously, scribes with a reputation for piety were often entrusted with this role. With their ability to manipulate the interpretations of the Law to their advantage, the system was rife with abuse.

Throughout Scripture, widows were portrayed as the supreme examples of the destitute and powerless (today's first reading from 1 Kings is an example). Jesus again makes a considerable impact on his hearers, then, by lifting up a widow who has nothing as an example of faithful generosity. Only that which is given not from our abundance but from our own need and poverty — and given totally, completely, humbly and joyfully — is a gift fitting for God.

The widow's coin in today's Gospel can take many forms: a warm coat given to the poor, an hour spent each week teaching religious education to children, a quilt made to raise money for a worthy cause, a pan of lasagna. The widow's mite is "mighty" indeed, accomplishing great things not because of the size of the gift but because of the love and compassion that motivates the giver. In the Gospel scheme of things, it is not the measure of the gift but the measure of the love, selflessness and joy that directs the gift that is great before God. For Christ calls us not to seek greater things or talents to astound the world but for greater love and selflessness with which to enrich the world.

The kingdom of God is realized first in our embracing Christ's spirit of servanthood — servanthood that finds fulfillment and satisfaction in the love, compassion and kindness we can extend to others, that enables us to place the common good and the needs of others above our own wants and narrow interests.

Greatness in the reign of God is not measured by what is in our portfolios, bank accounts or resumes, but by the love in our hearts that directs the use and sharing of those gifts. The faithful disciple honors the dignity of the servant above the power of the rich, canonizes humility over celebrity and is inspired by the total generosity of the widow rather than the empty gestures of the scribe.

May we seek to lead and follow in the spirit of Jesus: to reveal the "footprint" of God's compassion in our own seeking of reconciliation rather than vengeance, justice rather than convention, selflessness rather than self-interest.

O God, Giver of all good things,
re-make our hearts in gratitude.
Humbled by your immeasurable goodness
and inspired by your Son's humble generosity
  while among us,
may we be always ready
to give, to heal, to comfort, to lift up
in the spirit of the widow's pennies —
from our own poverty,
despite our own need,
in joy that we are able to give,
humbled by your blessings that enable us
  to give.

Sunday 33

"Learn a lesson from the fig tree. When its branch becomes tender and sprouts leaves, you know that summer is near. In the same way, when you see these things happening, know that the Son of Man is near … Heaven and earth will pass away, but my words will not pass away."

Mark 13: 24–32
[Roman lectionary]

Changing worlds and passing stages

She sits at her laptop trying to summarize on a single page her young life thus far and "market" her still untested abilities. Just a few weeks ago she had typed out her senior thesis on these same keys; now she was firing off letters, resumes and applications for that all important first job. The safe stage of classes, research, term papers and final exams has passed; the college graduate takes her first steps on to the bigger — and frightening — stage of the marketplace.

The relationship is over; the parting may have been tragic, sudden, painfully lingering, bittersweet, acrimonious. But the reality must now be faced: the survivor has to continue on without the spouse he or she had always expected to be there forever. The world of two hearts made one has passed; a new world must be faced alone.

With the help of her daughter, she puts the last of her treasures in a carton, and her son-in-law takes it out to the car with the other boxes. It seems like only yesterday that she and her late husband signed the papers to purchase the house on Bartlett Street. Three children, two dogs, three cats, and an assortment of animals from gerbils to lizards have been raised here; Christmases and Fourths of July, birthdays and first communions, graduations and engagements have been celebrated here; and every catastrophe that could befall a family — from serious illness to financial crisis — shook these walls but did not topple them. Now the children have homes and families of their own, her beloved husband has been dead for two years, and every day becomes a little more of a struggle for her. So the house on Bartlett Street has been sold and she has bought a small apartment in a beautiful assisted living community. She was surprised how happily she gave away so many things; it made her happy to know that her treasures would continue to bring joy and be useful to those she loved. Now, with a few cherished possessions and a third of the square footage, she begins the next chapter of her blessed life.

Life is a journey through changing worlds and passing stages. Change — sometimes frightening, often traumatic, always difficult — is part of that journey for all of us. From childhood, through adolescence, into adulthood and beyond, we are confronted by new "signs" of God's presence that, in challenging our self-centered view of the world, are opportunities for growth, maturity and understanding.

Chapter 13 of Mark's Gospel is Jesus' discourse on "the end" and the cataclysmic transformation from our time to the time of God (the first generation of Christians, for whom Mark is writing, expected the return of Christ in their own lifetimes). In the image of the fig tree, Jesus calls us to see faith in God as a prism for understanding and a tool for coping with the change that is part of every life. Christ promises that if we calibrate our compasses for the journey in the values of the Gospel, we will negotiate the turns and survive the obstacles along our way. The unsettling images Jesus articulates in today's Gospel confront us with the reality that the things we treasure — our careers, our portfolios, our bodies, our celebrity — will one day be no more and that our separation from them will be bitter.

The signs of the end times should not frighten us or terrify us into submission before the horrible wrath of God; Jesus urges us, instead, to recognize such "signs" in a spirit of hope and a perspective of faith in God's providence: to appreciate what a precious gift our limited time on earth is; to realize that every changing world and passing stage, every pain and triumph, are opportunities for growth, maturity and understanding of the transforming presence of God in one another; to embrace change — the passing away of our own "heaven and earth" — as part of our journey to the dwelling place of God.

With every change in direction, with every wrinkle of age, with every changing world and passing stage, we remain heirs to the promise of the Resurrection.

*H*elp us, O Lord,
to embrace the lesson of the "fig tree."
That we may seek the lasting harvest that we can reap through the planting
of compassion, reconciliation and justice.

Proper 28

"Do you see these great buildings? Not one stone will be left here upon another; all will be thrown down ... "

Mark 13: 1–8
[Common lectionary]

We made it ...

*F*or most of us, being a teenager seemed like a constant run-for-our-lives through no-man's land, dodging enemy bullets across a war-ravaged field. It was hard to keep up with the physical and emotional changes going on both outside and inside us. Along the way, we tripped any number of land-mines: break-ups, bad skin, fights with our parents (who just did NOT understand us), disasters in class. The expectations of teachers and coaches were greater and more exacting. And yet, we survived those difficult years: We learned from what we didn't know, we became wiser in the wake of disappointment and embarrassments, we realized the importance of responsibility and dependability.

(And to the teenagers among us: You, too, will survive your high school and college years.)

That first job after college can be exhilarating and terrifying at the same time. We wondered if we're cut out for this career. We doubted our abilities. We wished we had listened and worked harder in that economics or writing course. We couldn't understand why our boss was such a jerk. And yet, we found ways to survive and even move forward: We worked hard, we paid attention, we were taken under the wing of a wise co-worker or mentor — maybe even a smart boss who remembered what it was like when he or she had started out.

(And if you're just starting out, trust us: You'll make it, too.)

Are we ever really ready for marriage and a family of our

own? Can this person really love me — forever?! Shouldn't there be some kind of official certification or course in how to be a parent? Should I be raising a child — when I still feel like a kid myself? And yet, we manage to survive — and our kids survive, too. Oh, it's not easy. From the pile of diapers to the mountain of bills, from the chaos at mealtimes to the battles over homework and video games, from the constant dashing from after-school music lessons to weekend sports, it can all be overwhelming. But together, you and your spouse continue to love and trust and honor the gifts each of you bring to create your happy and welcoming home.

Despite the terrifying images of war and disasters, today's Gospel is one of hope and reassurance. Jesus promises us that faith in the God of all that is good provides us with the tools and resources to survive whatever gauntlet life forces us to run.

We all live every day in the shadow of eternity. With every experience of loss, with every sign of illness, with every hint of age creeping upon us, we become more and more aware of our mortality. In chapter 13 of Mark's Gospel, Jesus predicts times of trial and destruction. In the Roman lectionary, the final verses of Chapter 13 — the parable of the fig tree — are read today (see above). Communities using the common lectionary hear the opening verses of Mark 13. Jesus warns that the end of all things is inevitable — but that such destruction is the beginning of the kingdom of God.

The first generation of Christians expected Christ to return in their lifetimes. When their world began to collapse around them under the Roman onslaught of Jerusalem (including the destruction of the temple, as Jesus predicts, in 70 A.D.), they wondered in their anguish, *When will Jesus return for us?* Jesus does not deny the pain and anguish of the end (citing in today's Gospel reading the graphic images of the prophet Daniel) nor that the earth will indeed pass away. But the important thing is not when Jesus will come (for we know he will), but our readiness to meet him. Preparation, not panic, is the Christ-centered response to such change.

There are signs all around us — like the late autumn winds of November — that remind us that we live in the shadow of eternity. Every "stone" we set in our lives, no matter how painstakingly set, will, at some time, "be thrown down." Jesus urges us to recognize such "signs" with eyes and spirits of faith: to appreciate what a precious gift our limited time on earth is; to realize that every changing world and passing stage, every pain and triumph, are opportunities for growth, maturity and understanding of the transforming presence of God in one another; to embrace change as part of our journey to the dwelling place of God.

In life's most difficult crises and in the fear and despair of responding to those crises, God remains present to us in the goodness within ourselves and in the caring compassion offered by others. In the wars we fight, the earthquakes that shake our sureties, the disasters that topple our secure self-centered worlds, we can always rebuild our lives on the stronger and timeless things of God: compassion, reconciliation, friendship, generosity.

 God,
may we come to appreciate this gift of life
and the precious time you have given us.
In the days and years you give us,
in the changes we experience,
may we journey in hope,
despite our fears and despair
to your dwelling place beyond this time.

Christ the King /
The Reign of Christ [Proper 29]

"For this I was born, and for this I came into the world, to testify to the truth. Everyone who belongs to the truth listens to my voice."

John 18: 33–37

Welcome to Jesus' place ...

*E*very evening you and your family gather around the table in your kitchen for supper. The entree might be some epicurean delight from the pages of *Bon Appétit* — but more often than not it's Chinese takeout or pizza from the corner pizzeria. As everyone digs in, the table buzzes with talk of tomorrow's soccer game, a crabby teacher, the current fix-up project, the latest office crises, and a new knock-knock joke. Here at the kitchen table, parent and child give and receive encouragement, consolation, forgiveness and love. Especially love. If there is one safe harbor on earth, one secure, sheltered place where you are always welcome no matter how badly you mess up, the kitchen table is it. Your kitchen — the place where Christ reigns.

A storm or earthquake devastates a town; a fire reduces a neighborhood to burnt timber and ashes; an act of terrorism cuts a wide and bloody swath through a village. That's when they go to work: skilled medical professionals, tireless construction workers, patient and gifted counselors, compassionate volunteers. These dedicated souls work around the clock to care for the hurt and injured, rescue those in danger, help the traumatized cope, and begin the hard work of rebuilding. By their very presence, these good people transform the debris and ashes into the kingdom of Jesus.

The tired old downtown building has seen better days but no better use. The city's churches have banded together to turn the brick structure into a community center, a safe place where children can come to play basketball, receive tutoring, or just hang out after school. The well-stocked pantry provides for dozens of hungry families every week; a free clinic offers basic on-site medical care and referral services to the poor and uninsured. Its meeting rooms are always busy: the elderly have a place to go for companionship and immigrants are taught how to master the language of their new homeland. In this austere brick building, Jesus rules.

The kingdom of Jesus is not found in the world's centers of power but within human hearts; it is built not by deals among the power elite but by compassionate hands; Christ reigns neither by influence nor wealth but by generosity and justice.

We celebrate the kingship of Jesus with John's Gospel account of what is perhaps Jesus' most humiliating moment: his appearance before Pilate. It is an extraordinary exchange: Pilate has been blackmailed by the Jewish establishment into executing Jesus for their ends — but it is the accused who dominates the meeting and takes on the role of inquisitor.

Pilate, a man of no great talent or competence, was under a great deal of political pressure. He had needlessly alienated the Jews of Palestine by his cruelty, his insensitivity to their religious customs and his clumsy appropriation of funds from the temple treasury for public projects. Reports of his undistinguished performance had reached his superiors in Rome. Pilate has no idea what this Jesus is talking about regarding "truth" or a kingdom built of compassion, humility and justice.

This is all well above Pilate's pay grade.

While a politician and "powerful" figure like Pilate cannot grasp the "kingship" of Jesus, we who have been baptized in the life, death and resurrection of Christ are called to build and maintain that kingdom in our own time and place. Christ's reign is realized only in our embracing a vision of humankind as a family made in the image of God, a vision of one another as brothers and sisters in Christ, a vision of the world centered in the spirit of hope and compassion taught by Christ.

Christ's reign is realized only in our embracing a vision of humankind as a family made in the image of God, a vision of one another as brothers and sisters in Christ, a vision of the world centered in the spirit of hope and compassion taught by Christ.

*C*hrist of compassion, Lord of reconciliation,
you have entrusted to us the work
  of completing your kingdom.
May our embracing your spirit of selflessness,
may our imitating your compassionate servanthood,
reveal your presence in our midst
and establish your reign of justice and peace
in this time and place
as we journey throughout our lives
to the perfection of your rule
in the kingdom of your Father.

Notes

Christmas

1. From *A Thomas Merton Reader*, edited by Thomas P. McDonnell (New York: Image Books, 1974, 1989), pages 155, 156, 157.

Lent

1. From "Beckoned by the Desert: An antidote to subjective spirituality" by Alan F. Simek, *America*, June 18–25, 2007.

2. Adapted from *Breast Cancer Husband: How to Help You Wife (and Yourself) Through Diagnosis, Treatment and Beyond*, by Marc Silver (Rodale Books, 2004).

Easter Triduum

1. From "Remembering When: What If Alzheimer's someday robs my husband of our memories?" by Brooke Lea Foster, *The Boston Sunday Globe Magazine*, April 12, 2009.

Easter

1. From *Overcoming Life's Disappointments*, by Rabbi Harold S. Kushner (New York: Alfred A. Knopf, 2006), page 46.

2. *Traveling Mercies: Some Thoughts on Faith* by Anne Lamott (New York: Pantheon Books, 1999), pages 100, 101.

3. From "Labors of Love" by Lawrence Wood, *The Christian Century*, May 17, 2003. Used with permission.

4. *Roots* by Alex Haley (Garden City, New York: Doubleday & Company, 1974), pages 578–579.

Solemnities of the Lord in Ordinary Time

1. From *Once Upon a Time in Africa: Stories of Wisdom and Joy*, compiled by Joseph G. Healey (New York: Orbis Books, 2005), pages 19–20.

2. From "What's In a Kiss?" by Mary Ann Rollano, *Spirituality & Health*, November/December 2005.

Ordinary Time

1. Adapted from *When the Rain Speaks: Celebrating God's Presence in Nature* by Sister Melanie Svoboda, S.N.D. (Twenty-Third Publications, 2008), page 14.

2. From "What's In a Kiss?" by Mary Ann Rollano, *Spirituality & Health*, November/December 2005.

3. *Never Have Your Dog Stuffed — And Other Things I've Learned*, by Alan Alda (New York: Random House, 2005), page 151.

4. From "My Life as a Statistic" by Steve Maas, *The Boston Globe Magazine*, December 7, 2008.

5. Sue Diaz, writing in *Child Magazine* (August 1994). Used with permission of the author.

6. From *My Grandfather's Blessings: Stories of Strength, Refuge and Belonging*, by Rachel Naomi Remen, M.D. (New York: Riverhead Books, 2000), pages 1–2.

7. From "A driving-purposed life" by Nancy Kennedy, *Catholic Digest*, April 2009.

8. Reprinted with permission from *At Home With Our Faith*, May 2002, Claretian Publications (www.homefaith.com, 800/328–6515).

9. *Iran Awakening: A Memoir of Revolution and Hope*, by Shirin Ebadi and Azadek Maveni (Random House, 2006), pages xv–xvi.

10. Scott Russell Sanders, *Staying Put: Making a Home in a Restless World* (Boston: Beacon Press, 1994) page 35.

11. From "A Thief in the Night" by Valerie Schultz, *America*, February 27, 2006.

12. Catherine O'Connell-Cahill, *At Home With Our Faith*, Claretian Publications, September 2007.

13. From a sermon by the Rev. Dennis Maynard [www.Episkopols.com].

14. *My Monastery Is a Minivan: Where the Daily is Divine and the Routine Becomes Prayer*, by Denise Roy (Chicago: Loyola Press, 2001), pages 182, 183.

15. From "When all we need is a listener" by Elissa Ely, *The Boston Globe*, May 31, 2009.

16. From "The Best Teaching I Ever Got for a Buck" by Melissa Hart, *Spirituality & Health*, March/April 2003.